Courage, Respect and Assertiveness

A Lucky Duck Book

Enhancing Courage, Respect and Assertiveness

Karen Brunskill

P·C·P
Paul Chapman
Publishing

First published 2006

Originally published in Australia as Values for Life Upper Level Primary Series One 2002

 Paul Chapman Publishing
A SAGE Publications Company
1 Oliver's Yard
55 City Road
London EC1Y 1SP

SAGE Publications Inc.
2455 Teller Road
Thousand Oaks, California 91320

SAGE Publications India Pvt Ltd.
B-42, Panchsheel Enclave
Post Box 4109
New Delhi 110 017

www.luckyduck.co.uk

Commissioning Editor: George Robinson
Editorial Team: Mel Maines, Sarah Lynch, Wendy Ogden
Designer: Nick Shearn
Illustrations: Leanne Winfield, Katie Jardine, Helen Sylvester, Michael Dell, Lori Head, Claire Saxby, Jacquie Young, Helen Miles, Ian Moule, Jennifer Cooke

A catalogue record for this book is available from the British Library
Library of Congress Control Number 2006900194

ISBN13 978-1-4129-1964-7
ISBN10 1-4129-1964-9 (pbk)

Printed on paper from sustainable resources
Printed in Great Britain by The Cromwell Press Ltd, Trowbridge, Wiltshire

The CD-ROM contains PDF files, labelled 'Worksheets.pdf' which consists of the stories and worksheets for each lesson in this resource. You will need Acrobat Reader version 3 or higher to view and print these resources.

The documents are set up to print to A4 but you can enlarge them to A3 by increasing the output percentage at the point of printing using the page set-up settings for your printer.

Contents

The *Promoting Children's Resilience and Wellbeing* series were originally published in Australia as the *Values for Life* series of books, and when we saw them we felt they would provide valuable additions to our range of books on emotional literacy. One of the attractions was that the four books provided a coherent programme from early years through to 12.

Book 1: *Learning to be Honest, Kind and Friendly* (Age range: 5 to 7)

Book 2: *Learning to be Confident, Determined and Caring* (Age range: 5 to 7)

Book 3: *Developing Consideration, Respect and Tolerance* (Age range: 7 to 9)

Book 4: *Enhancing Courage, Respect and Assertiveness* (Age range: 9 to 12)

In Australia the term 'emotional resilience' is more widely used than in the UK, though the term is increasingly current here. Resilience is the ability to recover from adversity or difficult situations or circumstances. Fuller (2001) suggests that life events are 'contagious'. Life events, both positive and negative, establish chains of behaviour. If children are faced with negative events their interpretation of these events will influence how they cope. If they don't have resilience they are likely to react in a negative way.

An example of a negative or risk chain would be:

> a child who grows up in violent circumstances and learns to distrust others, enters school and interprets the intention of others as hostile. The child then acts warily or aggressively towards peers and develops peer relationship problems…

An example of a positive or protective chain would be:

> a child who grows up in violent circumstances but learns, on entry to school, that there is a trustworthy adult who can be relied on to assist in the resolution of peer relationship difficulties. The child's positive attempts to interact with others are acknowledged. The child begins to feel accepted, mixes more appropriately with peers and develops a diversity of friendships. (Fuller, 2001)

The work of Goleman (1995) indicates that the promotion of protective factors in school life is not only predictive of academic success but even more importantly for positive adult life outcomes.

The idea of positive factors that promote resilience has been supported by research (Resnick, Harris and Blum, 1993; Fuller, McGraw and Goodyear, 1998). The main factors appear to be:

▸ family connectedness

▸ peer connectedness

▸ fitting in at school.

Two of these can be directly influenced by school life, creating positive experiences that are 'contagious'.

Resilience seems to depend largely on this sense of belonging. Once one belongs, empathy can develop and empathy builds group cohesion where moral actions such as honesty, altruism and caring emerge developmentally as the child matures.

This idea of resilience can be seen to be important in all areas of school life, as quoted in Fuller (2001):

> When schools promote belonging and ensure high levels of involvement between staff and students, bullying is reduced. (Citing the work of Olweus, 1995; Rigby 1996.)

This series, with its progressive programme, allows the opportunity for young people to explore:

- consideration
- honesty
- responsibility
- confidence

- courage
- caring
- friendliness
- kindness

- tolerance
- respect
- determination
- assertiveness.

As children mature the level that these can be explored becomes deeper; their reasoning and morality becomes more sophisticated with age and this type of programme can assist in their 'connectedness'. Our increasing awareness of the concept of 'Citizenship' should recognise elements such as empathy, moral reasoning and moral behaviour.

Current UK initiatives

The Healthy Schools Programme identifies emotional health and wellbeing (including bullying) as one of the areas schools have to develop and are required to produce evidence that they have met the necessary criteria. The Healthy Schools Programme, of course, is not a separate entity divorced from all other aspects of school development. The statutory components of PSHE and Citizenship for primary schools can be linked to the concept of emotional health and wellbeing and, we would also argue, emotional resilience.

The 12 domains covered in this programme fit the four components of PSHE and Citizenship at Key Stage 1 and 2:

1. Developing confidence and responsibility and making the most of their abilities.

2. Preparing to play an active role as citizens.

3. Developing a healthy, safer lifestyle.

4. Developing good relationships and respecting the difference between people.

The introduction of developing children's social, emotional and behavioural skills (SEBS) also highlights the importance of the type of material presented in this book.

- Emotional and social competence have been shown to be more influential than cognitive abilities for personal, career and scholastic success.

- Programmes that teach social and emotional competences have been shown to result in a wide range of educational gains.

- Work and workplace increasingly focus on social and emotional competences with increased emphasis on teamwork, communication, management skills etc. (DfES, 2003)

Though resilience is not mentioned directly, SEBS clearly identifies the earlier point about the 'contagious' effects of life events.

> Research is bringing home the wide extent of various types of neglect and abuse. This is being exacerbated by the breakdown of extended family and communities which reduces support for the nuclear family, and the higher rates of divorce and subsequent one-parent families. This has led to a shake-up in belief that we can leave children's emotional and social development to parents... so schools have to provide the emotional and social guidance that some pupils currently lack. (DfES, 2003)

However, helping young people develop emotional resilience isn't just for young people from disturbed or disturbing backgrounds. School life and home life can be stressful for all young people, and with the growing awareness of the importance of emotional literacy, the *Promoting Children's Resilience and Wellbeing* series will be an ideal programme to support a key element, emotional resilience.

George Robinson and Barbara Maines

Enhancing Courage, Respect and Assertiveness is made up of teacher's notes, copiable stories and student activity sheets.

The teacher's notes:

▶ outline the programme, its rationale and relationship to curriculum outcomes

▶ provide ideas about introducing each topic via the relevant story, class and individual activities, discussion, role-play and extension exercises.

The values and story titles introduced in the programme are:

	Value	Title
1.	Consideration	Kelly's Choice
2.	Friendliness	The Fisher Girl
3.	Honesty	The Biggest Whopper
4.	Kindness	Sophie's Gift
5.	Responsibility	Stinky Josh
6.	Tolerance	Sock It To Me Sam!
7.	Confidence	Prince Alex's Nose
8.	Respect	All Shapes and Sizes
9.	Courage	Samuel The Brave
10.	Determination	Streaky Road Dash
11.	Caring	Nan's Place
12.	Assertiveness	Slugger

Schools are a major area for social interaction, making them vital environments for primary prevention programmes based on the framework of reducing risk and promoting protective factors in the lives of students. Primary prevention is about building belonging, and promoting the wellbeing of all students.

This programme is designed to assist students to understand the core prosocial values that support the development of a safe and positive learning environment, social connectedness and wellbeing.

Listed below are five protective factors that assist in promoting resilience and wellbeing in young people (Hawkins and Catalano et al., 1996).

1. To assist students to feel a sense of belonging and fitting in at school.

2. To identify a special talent or interest for which he/she is recognised and encouraged.

3. To promote proactive problem-solving.

4. To enhance a positive social orientation.

5. To encourage an optimistic sense of future.

Each of the Value topics within the programme are mapped against some of the identified protective factors.

VALUE AND STORY TITLE	Sense of belonging and fitting in	Recognition of a special talent or gift	Promoting proactive problem solving	Enhance positive social orientation.	Encourage an optimistic sense of future.
CONSIDERATION Kelly's Choice	✔		✔	✔	✔
FRIENDLINESS The Fisher Girl	✔	✔	✔	✔	✔
HONESTY The Biggest Whopper	✔		✔	✔	
KINDNESS Sophie's Gift	✔	✔	✔	✔	✔
RESPONSIBILITY Stinky Josh	✔		✔	✔	✔
TOLERANCE Sock It To Me Sam!	✔	✔	✔		✔
CONFIDENCE Prince Alex's Nose	✔	✔	✔	✔	✔
RESPECT All Shapes and Sizes	✔		✔	✔	
COURAGE Samuel The Brave	✔		✔		✔
DETERMINATION Streaky Road Dash	✔	✔	✔	✔	
CARING Nan's Place	✔	✔		✔	
ASSERTIVENESS Slugger	✔	✔	✔	✔	✔

The programme may be used:

▸ To assist in the implementation of prosocial values and associated behaviours that help promote a safe and supportive whole school environment conducive to learning.

▸ To assist in the identification and development of a 'Language' of values and associated behaviours that promote student connectedness and engagement.

▸ To assist in the identification and development of social competence (bridging and bonding) and communication skills.

▸ To assist in the building of positive relationships with others, thus promoting emotional and social wellbeing.

▸ To assist in the promotion of protective factors that enhance resilience.

▸ To assist in the development, recognition and reinforcement of positive regard.

▸ To assist in the implementation of the school's Health and Wellbeing programmes, working in the areas of both prevention and early intervention.

▸ As a resource that promotes discussion and group work.

▸ To assist in the promotion and development of strong school and parent/home links.

The topics may be dealt with sequentially or as individual units of work, depending on the teacher's and students' needs.

The stories within each unit have been designed to be read by the class teacher or facilitator. Alternatively, multiple copies of a story can be used for group reading.

The individual stories take approximately ten minutes to read. The time taken to complete each unit will vary according to the depth with which each topic is examined, the activities undertaken and the level of student participation.

Title: Kelly's Choice

Main Focus Value of the Story: Consideration

Related Values to the Story

- Responsibility
- Honesty
- Determination
- Caring

Health and Wellbeing Outcomes

- Examining the influence of the media and peer pressure on health goals and behaviours.
- Examining the need to belong to a group.
- Exploring the benefits and risks of legal drug use (e.g. tobacco, alcohol) and discussing the impact these drugs may have on the body.
- Developing strategies that promote healthy choices.

Title: The Fisher Girl

Main Focus Value of the Story: Friendliness

Related Values to the Story

- Assertiveness
- Confidence
- Respect
- Kindness
- Helpfulness

Health and Wellbeing Outcomes

- Identifying feelings of safety and security.
- Identifying the behaviours that support friendliness.
- Encouraging a sense of belonging.
- Identifying individual talents and qualities.
- Examining advantages and disadvantages of stereotyping.
- Identifying major transitions in life.

Title: The Biggest Whopper

Main Focus Value of Story: Honesty

Related Values to the Story

- Responsibility
- Courage
- Respect
- Determination

Health and Wellbeing Outcomes

- Deciding right from wrong
- Identifying major influences on behaviour towards others' property
- Examining the impact of peer pressure on decision-making and laws
- Identifying strategies for responding to potentially dangerous or unsafe situations or activities.

Title: Sophie's Gift

Main Focus Value of the Story: Kindness

Related Values to the Story

- Helpfulness
- Tolerance
- Honesty
- Assertiveness
- Generosity
- Determination

Health and Wellbeing Outcomes

- Examining the way stereotypes are presented in the community and describing the advantages and disadvantages of defining people in terms of a stereotype.
- Identifying major influences on safety and personal health.
- Examining the impact that an act of kindness may have on another's life.

Title: Stinky Josh

Main Focus Value of the Story: Responsibility

Related Values to the Story

- Respect
- Consideration
- Honesty
- Caring
- Cleanliness
- Courtesy

Health and Wellbeing Outcomes

- Identifying major influences on health
- Identifying physical, social and emotional changes that are common to both sexes during puberty.
- Identifying the importance of taking responsibility for personal hygiene, and possible consequences of neglecting it.

Title: Sock It To Me Sam!

Main Focus Value of the Story: Tolerance

Related Values of the Story

- Respect
- Friendliness
- Patience
- Honesty
- Trust
- Helpfulness

Health and Wellbeing Outcomes

- Identifying differing family expectations, roles and responsibilities and how these affect relationships.
- How tolerance of differences impacts upon relationships.
- Examining the importance of setting goals to achieve an outcome.
- Identifying the roles that positive thinking and optimism play in achievements.

Title: Prince Alex's Nose

Main Focus Value of the Story: Confidence

Related Values to the Story

- Tolerance
- Friendliness
- Patience
- Caring
- Consideration

Health and Wellbeing Outcomes

- Examining the influence of media and peer pressure on behaviours
- Examining the need to belong to a group.
- Describing how meeting challenges may increase feelings of self-esteem and confidence.

Title: All Shapes and Sizes

Main Focus Value of the Story: Respect

Related Values to the Story

- Confidence
- Tolerance
- Helpfulness
- Courage
- Self-discipline

Health and Wellbeing Outcomes

▸ Examining the influence of the media and peer pressure on health goals and behaviours.

▸ Examining the need to belong to a group.

▸ Identifying major influences on personal health and wellbeing.

Title: Samuel The Brave

Main Focus Value of the Story: Courage

Related Values to the Story

▸ Caring

▸ Helpfulness

▸ Determination

▸ Reliability

Health and Wellbeing Outcomes

▸ Examining the way stereotypes are presented in the community and describing the advantages and disadvantages of defining people in terms of stereotypes.

▸ Identifying major influences on feelings of safety and security.

Title: Streaky Road Dash

Main Focus Value of Story: Determination

Related Values to the Story

▸ Courage

▸ Confidence

▸ Fairness

▸ Enthusiasm

Health and Wellbeing Outcomes

▸ Deciding right from wrong.

▸ Identifying major influences on behaviour towards others.

▸ Examining the impact of peer pressure on decision making.

Title: Nan's Place

Main Focus Value of Story: Caring

Related Values to the Story

▸ Responsibility

▸ Kindness

▸ Respect

▸ Tolerance

Health and Wellbeing Outcomes

▸ Identifying major influences on health.

- ▸ Identifying feelings of safety and security.
- ▸ Encouraging a sense of belonging.
- ▸ Identifying behaviours that enhance relationships.

Title: Slugger

Main Focus Value of Story: Assertiveness

Related Values to the Story

▸ Confidence	▸ Helpfulness
▸ Respect	▸ Patience

Health and Wellbeing Outcomes

- ▸ Identifying feelings of safety and security.
- ▸ Encouraging a sense of belonging.
- ▸ Identifying individual talents and qualities.
- ▸ Identifying behaviours that enhance relationships.

Structure of the Programme

Each section introduces a Focus Value and has the following format:

- ▸ **Focus Value**
- ▸ **Objectives**
- ▸ **Factors Enhancing Resilience**
- ▸ **Introduction to the Focus Value** – definition brainstormed by students; discussion on how the value and related behaviours could be positively demonstrated in school.
- ▸ **The Story** – read by the class teacher or copied for individual students; class discussion and related questions.
- ▸ **Activities** – three or four copiable activity sheets related to the value. These may involve:
  1. Small group tasks.
  2. Role-play scenarios.
  3. Individual student application to a task.
  4. Partner work.

Focus Values

Objectives

- To help students examine the influence of the media and peer pressure on health goals and behaviours.

- To help students identify the risks and benefits of legal drugs (e.g. paracetamol, tobacco, alcohol). To consider the facts about their use and discuss strategies for healthy choices.

- To help students examine the impact some habits may have on their long-term wellbeing.

- To help students examine the importance of consideration.

Factors Enhancing Resilience

- Promoting a sense of belonging and fitting in.

- Promoting proactive problem-solving.

- Enhancing a positive social orientation.

Introduction to the Focus Value

Brainstorm with the students and create a class definition of the focus value, 'consideration'. The students may like to use a dictionary or thesaurus to assist in defining the meaning. With the whole class or in small groups, discuss how the value of consideration could be positively demonstrated in the classroom and the playground, and how they would know it was not.

The Story: Kelly's Choice

The story may be read to the students by the class teacher, or in small groups if multiple copies have been made. Follow the story with a class discussion. Some suggested questions are:

- Why was Kelly's grandpa in hospital?

- Why was Kelly's dad annoyed with Grandpa?

- How did Kelly's grandpa start smoking? What did he regret about being a smoker? What do you think Grandpa wished he had considered before taking up smoking?

- What are some of the methods Kelly's mum used to give up smoking? Why do some people make excuses about giving up?

- How have attitudes to smoking changed over the years?

- What sort of peer pressure was Kelly put under at school to start smoking? How did she stand up for what she thought was right? What does being 'assertive' mean?

- Kelly realised Grandpa had to decide to quit for himself. Why?

- Why do some people encourage others to join them in smoking?

- What facts do you know about cigarette smoking and its impact on the body?

Materials

- Anatomy of a Cigarette Smoker activity sheet.

- Consider the Facts activity sheet.

- Consider the Outcome activity sheet.

- Pens, card and A3 paper.

- Paper bags or socks.

Kelly's Choice

Written by Leanne Winfield
Illustrated by Katie Jardine

Chapter 1

Kelly and her dad were visiting her Grandpa in hospital. Inside the white and grey building, it was warm and smelt funny. They walked up the steps and down a long hallway. Kelly looked into her grandpa's room and saw him sitting up in bed beside the window. He looked older and smaller than she remembered and his hair seemed greyer. He gasped when he breathed in and relaxed as if it was a relief when he breathed out. There was one other bed in the room, which was occupied by a restless, snoring man about Grandpa's age.

'How are you, Grandpa?' Kelly asked.

'Not bad, Kelly. It's good to see you and your dad.'

'When will you be coming home?'

'Not for a while yet,' he said. 'I need to have a rest. I've got pneumonia again. It'll take some time for me to get over it.'

'What is that packet of cigarettes doing on your bedside table?' Dad asked Grandpa. 'You told me you'd given up.'

'I have given up. They must be Charlie's. Hey, Charlie,' Grandpa called to the man in the other bed. 'What are your cigarettes doing on my bedside table? Here, catch!' He threw the packet to Charlie. Charlie picked it up as if he had never seen it before and then he lay back down and continued to doze noisily.

'I'm going to have a word with your doctor if I can find him,'

Dad said. 'Stay here, Kelly, and keep Grandpa company.'

'That's your brand of cigarettes, Grandpa,' Kelly said to him.

'You notice too much, young lady.'

'How can you be smoking when you're having trouble breathing?'

'It's ridiculous, I know. I feel like a kid again, hiding behind the bike shed, sneaking out when the nurse is not looking.'

'Where do you go to have a cigarette? You can't smoke in here.'

'Ernie and I go out the front with all the other smokers.'

'Grandpa, you should stop it. It's bad for you.'

'I'd like to, but I've been doing it for so long that I don't know how to stop. I'm so used to having the nicotine that I feel sick if I don't have it.'

'Mum gave up. Why can't you?'

'I've been smoking for a lot longer than your mother. She had hypnotherapy, nicotine patches, nicotine chewing gum and did the Quit programme. Most of that costs money; money that I don't have.'

But you can afford to buy cigarettes, Kelly thought.

'How did you start smoking, Grandpa?'

'When I was twelve, my brother Jamie and I used to pinch fags from our dad to share with the other lads in the street. At first it started off as a bit of a lark. The next thing I knew, we were doing it everyday. Nearly everyone smoked back then. Although it was known that it was bad for people's health, no one took any notice. There were ads on the telly, in the newspapers and in magazines, advertising cigarettes. All the movie stars smoked.'

'Did you want to smoke? Why didn't you say no?' asked Kelly.

'I didn't think about it. I went along with the crowd.'

'Do you wish that you hadn't?'

'I would have saved a lot of money, that's for sure. And I'd probably feel a lot better right now and recover from pneumonia much more quickly. Why are you asking all these questions, Kelly?'

Chapter 2

Kelly thought back to lunch-time at school. She and her best friend, Melissa, had been sitting on the benches at the back of the school ground talking about what had happened on television the night before. Jessica and her friends had walked up to them.

'This is our spot,' Jessica said. 'The teachers can't see us here. You either join in or go somewhere else.'

'What do you mean?' Melissa asked.

'This is the smokers' spot.'

'It's never been the smokers' spot before. Why is it now?' questioned Melissa.

'It just is, okay. So if you stay here, you have to smoke.'

'I don't want to smoke,' Kelly said. 'Anyway, we don't have any,' said Melissa.

'Well we're not giving you any. You have to bring your own. Go away and don't come back unless you're joining the group.'

'Come on, Melissa. Let's go.' Kelly led Melissa off to sit on the grass in the shade of the gum tree near the monkey bars.

'We should get some cigarettes,' Melissa said. 'Jessica's really cool. I think we should join her group.'

'No. I don't want to smoke. Mum used to smoke in the house before she gave up. It stinks. It gets in your hair and in your clothes. Yugh! It's awful,' replied Kelly.

'How do you know you don't want to do it, if you haven't tried it?' asked Melissa.

'I don't need to try it. I passive smoked at home for years! I don't want to, Melissa. Don't make a big deal about this. You're not really thinking about it. Jessica has never wanted to be friends with us before, why would she change her mind now?'

'You're being a drag, Kelly.'

As Kelly walked away from Melissa feeling frustrated and let down, the bell went. They didn't speak to each other for the rest of the day.

Chapter 3

Why am I asking all these questions of Grandpa? Kelly thought.

'There are some kids smoking at school, Grandpa. And I want you to get better. You should stop.'

'Yes, Kelly. I should stop. And don't you start, either.' They smiled at each other. Kelly's dad returned and he did not look happy.

'I've been speaking to the nurse, Dad. She said that you're not being cooperative. You have to take the tablets they give you and you've got to stop going outside the hospital to have a smoke. Just going outside with pneumonia is not good for you, let alone breathing in cigarette smoke.'

'There's nothing worse than a reformed smoker,' Grandpa snarled at Dad.

'Charlie, give me that packet,' Dad demanded.

Charlie had woken up and been following the argument between Dad and Grandpa as if it were a tennis match. He handed over the packet Grandpa had thrown to him earlier.

'Now come on, son. You could leave me at least some moments of enjoyment in this boring place.'

Kelly knew Grandpa was arguing for the sake of it. Maybe he had come around to another point of view, maybe he had a stash of cigarettes hidden away somewhere. In the end, it was his decision. She didn't want to spoil the visit and make him totally miserable; the idea had been to cheer him up. But Dad was on a roll.

'You know all about the awful health problems smoking causes. If you got gangrene you could lose a limb. Why would you risk that? And, what about cancer? Why would you put yourself through that? Come on, Dad. You've got to stop if you want to get better. Think about it. We'll be back tomorrow.'

Kelly gently kissed Grandpa on the cheek. She waved as she followed her father down the white and grey hallway.

Chapter 4

When Kelly and her dad arrived home Kelly's mother was in the kitchen cooking dinner. Kelly sat on the stool at the bench and watched her parents chop vegetables and prepare rice.

'My father is a stubborn old goat,' Kelly's dad told her mother.

'What's he doing now?'

'Smoking and not taking his medicine.'

'That sounds like your father!'

'That's not fair,' Kelly said. 'Both of you used to smoke.'

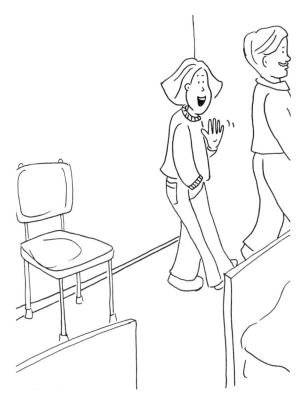

'Yes, but we made the effort to stop. It's not easy. But we did it. That's why it's better not to start.'

'Why did you give up, Mum?'

'Do you remember when Nana died? She was still fairly young. I wondered if she could have lived longer if she hadn't been a smoker. I was angry that she hadn't taken care of herself.

That's when I decided to stop.'

'We both stopped,' Kelly's father said. 'Best thing we've done for ages. Food tastes so much better as well.'

'Dinner's ready, let's eat.'

Chapter 5

The next day at school, Kelly met Melissa at the gate as usual.

'I don't want to fight, Melissa,' she said. 'Let's be friends.'

'Me too. I have missed you.'

At lunch-time, Kelly and Melissa sat on the grass in the shade of the oak tree beside the monkey bars. Kelly told Melissa about her visit to see her grandpa in hospital.

'I hope he gets better,' Melissa said.

'Me too,' said Kelly.

'I thought you two were coming to join us today.' It was Jessica and her friends.

'No, we're not,' Kelly told her.

'No.' said Melissa.

'You're a pair of wimps. Goody-two-shoes! We're going to give up on being friends with you!'

'Good, because we're going to give up on getting gangrene, bronchitis and lung cancer.'

'What are you talking about?' Jessica demanded. 'You're a pair of nutters.'

Kelly and Melissa laughed as Jessica and her friends walked away.

That afternoon, Kelly visited Grandpa again. She told him about the incident with Jessica.

'I'm proud of you, Kelly.' Then very quietly, as if it were a secret, he whispered to her, 'I quit yesterday. But don't tell your father. I want him to have something to complain about.'

'I'm proud of you too, Grandpa. You look better already.'

Activities and Discussion

Class Discussion

Introduce the topic to the students by suggesting that some of our behaviours may be influenced by the media and peer pressure even though we know that these behaviours may not be good health choices for us.

The class discussion can include questions such as:

▸ How do peers and the media try to influence our health choices? e.g. body image, clothing, hobbies, interests, behaviour, sayings, food, soft drinks.

▸ Brainstorm and make a class list about the things you consider before making your choices.

▸ What do you think influenced Kelly's grandpa to try smoking?

▸ What type of image did Jessica portray of smoking?

▸ How did Kelly perceive the group of teenagers when they were smoking in the story?

Good Health Choices

Working in small groups, design a television commercial promoting a good health choice. Create a catchy slogan or song to promote your concept. Focus on the concept of practising consideration for your body.

Alternatively, role-play a situation about positive health where someone has to make an informed choice, taking into consideration as many known facts as possible before making their decision.

Ask the students to complete the activity sheet The Anatomy of a Cigarette Smoker.

Consider the Facts

Ask the students to brainstorm and list as many legal drugs as they can (for example, tobacco, alcohol, paracetamol, asthma inhalant, insulin, antibiotics, cough syrup, and vitamins)

The students will need to be in small groups for cooperative discussion. Ask the groups to choose six legal drugs from the class list and complete the activity sheet Consider The Facts.

Ask the students to identify who (for example, a parent) would influence their decision to use the legal drug.

Each group is required to brainstorm and list everything they know to be true about each drug, including the benefits and risks associated with the use of these drugs.

The groups are then asked to list any questions they didn't know the answer to, for class discussion later. Once the groups are finished, they report their findings back to the class.

Consider the Outcome

Ask the students to devise a scenario that involves interaction between friends, where one person is being asked or pressured to do something potentially unsafe or risky. Ask them to take into consideration the possible impact of the decision upon the person's wellbeing.

Possible scenarios may include:

- friends wanting you to steal something from a shop
- friends telling you to lie to your parents about where you are going
- friends wanting you to have a cigarette
- friends wanting you to make a nasty phone call to another student in the class
- friends wanting you to do something that is illegal.

The group is to demonstrate two different outcomes:

1. The person under pressure does not know how to resolve the situation and succumbs to group pressure to participate even though they don't want to.

2. The person under pressure has a strategy or argument that allows them to resolve the problem while still retaining their friendships.

To reinforce points, at the conclusion of each scenario the teacher may lead a class discussion to help identify the strategies used by each group.

Ask the students to make the Response Cube on the activity sheet Consider The Outcome.

Legal Drug Use: Considerations

Ask the students to design a poster displaying some of the things people need to consider before they use legal drugs, for example, tobacco, alcohol or paracetamol.

Ask the students, in small groups to design a short puppet show highlighting some of the considerations to be taken into account before a decision is made in your area of choice.

Paper bag or sock puppets are easy to make and fun to work with. Alternatively, the students might like to develop their own type of puppet.

Anatomy of a Cigarette Smoker

In the space below, draw a diagram of a person and label as many effects that cigarette smoking has on the body as you can.

Consider the Facts

Our legal drugs:

1. ....
2. ....
3. ....
4. ....
5. ....
6. ....

Who would influence you to use these?

_____

_____

Brainstorm and list the benefits and risks for each drug.

_____

_____

_____

_____

_____

_____

_____

_____

For class discussion

List any questions you didn't know the answer to:

_____

_____

Any other discussion points regarding legal drugs:

_____

_____

_____

Consider the Outcome

On each face of the cube, write a possible response to your group's potentially unsafe or risky scenario.

Throw the cube and practise ways of responding to your scenario.

Objectives

▸ To help students to identify the various forms that bullying may take.

▸ To help students identify values and behaviours that promote a sense of belonging and a sense of safety.

▸ To help students examine the importance of friendliness.

Factors Enhancing Resilience

▸ Promoting a sense of belonging and fitting in.

▸ Recognition of a special talent or gift.

▸ Promoting proactive problem-solving.

▸ Encouraging an optimistic sense of future.

Introduction to the Focus Value

Brainstorm with the students and create a class definition of the focus value, 'friendliness'. The students may like to use a dictionary or thesaurus to assist in defining the meaning. With the whole class, or in small groups, discuss how the value of friendliness could be positively demonstrated in the classroom and the playground, and how they would know if it was not.

The Story: The Fisher Girl

The story may be read by the class teacher, or in small groups if multiple copies have been made.

Follow the story with a class discussion. Some suggested questions are:

▸ What is bullying?

▸ How was bullying behaviour portrayed in the story?

▸ What type of behaviours could be classified as bullying behaviours?

▸ Why do people bully?

▸ How would you react to a bullying incident from the story if you were one of the characters?

▸ What do you think are the effects of bullying behaviour on bullied students or bystanders?

▸ Why should we try not to bully each other?

▸ How would you have reacted in the story if you were Adam?

▸ What does friendly behaviour look like at school?

Materials

▸ Identifying Negative and Positive Behaviours activity sheet.

▸ Scenarios activity sheet.

▸ Feeling Valued activity sheet.

▸ Promoting Friendly Behaviour Brochure activity sheet.

▸ Coloured pens and glue.

▸ A3 paper and paper for brochures.

▸ Items for the Friendly Showbag.

Focus Value – Friendliness

The Fisher Girl

Written by Leanne Winfield
Illustrated by Katie Jardine

Chapter 1

'I'm really looking forward to my new job,' Mum said as she unpacked another box. 'No more city living. We'll be able to milk the cows, fish in the river and breathe fresh country air.'

'I don't want to milk cows, or fish or breathe fresh air,' Adam replied. 'I want to stay with Anna.'

'You'll still see Anna. She can stay with us during the holidays. You'll make new friends here.'

Adam didn't want new friends. He didn't want to go to a new school. He liked his old school, but he had no choice. The house had been sold and the furniture had been moved.

Chapter 2

On Monday morning, Adam's mother drove him to his new school and then took him to the office.

The office lady smiled at him. 'It's nice to have you here, Adam. I'm Mrs Barnes. I'll show you to your classroom.'

Mum kissed Adam on the cheek. 'Have a good day,' she said. Adam turned his face away. Mum smiled reassuringly at him and then dashed off to her car.

Adam followed Mrs Barnes down the hallway. It was a much newer and brighter building than his old school. Students' paintings were displayed all the way down the hallway and there were pegs outside the classrooms where students hung their bags and jackets. Much nicer than the old, worn benches he was used to.

Mrs Barnes introduced Adam to his teacher. Ms Smith was young, and she seemed to be relaxed and friendly.

She smiled at Adam. 'Welcome to 5S, S for Smith.'

Ms Smith was going to be a much nicer teacher than grumpy old Mr Harrison, Adam thought to himself.

'You can sit next to Sylvia today. I'll organise another desk tomorrow. Sylvia, will you show Adam around the school, please?'

'I'm not showing anyone around!' Sylvia declared gruffly.

Adam groaned. Sylvia didn't seem to be friendly at all.

'I'll show Adam around, Ms Smith,' said a boy with glasses, coming to the rescue.

'Fine, Kevin. Thank you. You need to learn some manners, Sylvia McRead. Adam, please sit beside Sylvia. She'll explain what we're doing.'

Adam smiled at Kevin and then scowled at Sylvia as he put his books on the desk and sat down.

'What are you doing?' he asked her.

'Nothing! Get lost. You're ugly. Where did you come from, Uglyville?' she said as she pushed his books off the desk.

What have I done? Adam thought. Quietly he picked up his books, deciding not to report her.

Looking over at her book, he noticed the page was blank. He looked at the book belonging to the student over the aisle. Her page was full of writing.

Ms Smith noticed that Sylvia wasn't helping Adam. 'We're writing about what we did on the weekend,' she said.

'Easy,' thought Adam, as he started to write about moving house.

He glanced over at Sylvia and noticed that she was drawing a beautiful, sparkling fish leaping off her page.

'I thought we were supposed to be writing,' Adam said.

'Mind your own business, Fatso. I do what I want,' Sylvia said as she thumped him on his arm.

'Ow!' he squeaked. 'That hurt. Don't you know it's not right to hit people?'

'Take this then, Dumbo.' Sylvia pinched him on the arm.

Just then the bell went for playtime. Kevin caught up with Adam as he was going out the door.

'Sylvia's awful. She's calling me names and pinching me. Do you think I should tell the teacher?' Adam asked.

'No. You'll be sitting at another desk tomorrow. Don't worry about her. Sylvia's just weird. Look at her over there. No one wants to play with her. Come on, let's go down to the football field.'

For the rest of that day, Sylvia continued to pinch, prod and insult Adam in class. He tried to ignore her, but every now and then he couldn't help reacting. He felt miserable.

At the end of the day, Kevin left to catch his bus. 'See you tomorrow,' he said. As Adam left the classroom, Sylvia rushed past him, dragging his school bag off his shoulder. She threw it in the mud as she dodged out of the school gate.

'See you tomorrow, Fishbait,' she called back over her shoulder laughing.

Adam picked up his muddy bag and sat on the bench outside the gate to wait for his mother. He felt like crying. He didn't want to come back to school tomorrow. How could he put up with more of Sylvia's treatment? The only good thing about the day had been meeting Kevin.

Chapter 3

Adam's mother pulled up in her car and leant out of the window.

'How was it? Let's go for a walk along the river. I'll buy you an ice cream when we get to the shop.'

Adam got into the car. He didn't feel like going to the river but it was better than going home and watching television.

'Okay. Let's walk along the riverside.'

'I had a fabulous day. I knew this job was going to be great. Best decision I ever made. Isn't this a wonderful place?' she asked as they got out of the car to walk along the riverside.

'Umm. Great, just great,' Adam replied. Should he tell his mother about his problem with Sylvia? 'I don't like this school, Mum.'

'What don't you like?'

'I had to sit next to a girl called Sylvia. She hit me and called me names.'

'Stand up for yourself, Adam. Tell her to leave you alone.'

'I did. She didn't take any notice.'

'It's only your first day. I'm sure things will get better. Did you meet anyone you like?'

'A boy called Kevin. We played together at lunch-time.'

'Great! You can invite him over on the weekend.'

They passed a number of people fishing and others out for a walk. Adam's mother stopped beside a girl and watched her put bait on her line. Adam didn't take much notice. He was looking for fish in the crystal clear water.

'Are you catching much?' his mother asked.

'Just a few trout,' a familiar voice replied. Adam shivered as he thought of the insults he had heard that voice utter during the day.

Turning around, he saw Sylvia sitting on the edge of the jetty, her legs dangling over the side. She was smiling at his mother. What a creep! Then she noticed him.

'What are you doing here?' she demanded.

'It's a free world. You don't own the riverside.'

'You two know each other! How lovely! I'm Adam's mum. Great! You've made friends,' she said as Adam rolled his eyes. 'You'll have to come over one afternoon. What's your name?'

'That's not a good idea, Mum. Sylvia's not my friend.'

'Nonsense. I'm sure she will be once you get to know each other.

We're going to have an ice cream. Sylvia, would you like to join us?'

'Yes, please,' she said, smirking at Adam.

After they'd eaten their ice creams, Mum said she had to go back into the shop to buy some things for dinner.

'Why don't you show Adam how to fish, Sylvia? I'm sure he'd love to learn.'

'Mum!'

'Right,' said Sylvia as Adam's mother walked back into the shop.

'Just watch out that I don't push you in,' she threatened with a laugh.

Great, thought Adam. Thumped and drowned all in one day.

'Sit here, watch and listen,' said Sylvia. Adam sat more than an arm's length away. 'This is the bait. You thread it onto the hook, like this. Some people use maggots but I prefer worms.'

'Where do you find the worms?' he asked.

'I dig them out of the garden at home. Then you cast, like this.' She demonstrated and then gave Adam the fishing rod. 'If you feel a tug, tell me. I'll set up the other line as well.'

'If there's a tug, does that mean there's a fish on the line?'

'Maybe, it could also be the fish nibbling at the bait. You have to be patient. After a while you get a feel for it, and you know when to reel it in. Sometimes, if you're too quick, the fish gets away.'

'I felt something!' Adam called out.

'All right, take it easy! Sit still for a moment. Tell me if you feel anything else.'

'There it is again. And again. Stronger this time.'

'Right! Yank the line up and start reeling it in. Quickly!'

Adam followed Sylvia's instructions and a moment later there was a fish dangling above the water. Adam reeled it in. It sparkled in the sunlight.

'Wow,' Adam said quietly. 'What sort is it?'

'It's a trout. A good size too.'

'Now what?' Adam asked.

'Take it off the hook. Perhaps I'd better show you,' she said, taking the rod from him. 'I can scale and fillet it for you if you'd like to take it home for dinner?'

'That would be great! Eating the first fish that I caught!' He watched as she efficiently cleaned and sliced the fish. She handed him two fillets in a spare plastic bag.

'Thanks, Sylvia. There's Mum in the car park. I'll see you tomorrow.'

As he ran down the riverside, Adam realised that Sylvia hadn't punched, pinched or insulted him once. In fact, she'd been very nice.

Chapter 4

The next morning, Adam kissed his mother goodbye in the car. He ran up to his classroom, looking for Sylvia. He finally found her outside the infants' area.

'Give me 50 pence and then you can go to your classroom,' Sylvia demanded. A small, scared boy looked up at her cautiously.

'I haven't got 50 pence,' the boy bravely told her.

'Make sure you bring it tomorrow! And you too, Dog-breath,' she said to another boy standing nearby.

'What are you doing, Sylvia?' Adam demanded. 'Leave these little kids alone. I'd just started to think that you're okay and here you are picking on these boys!'

'Get a life, Fishbait! Don't tell me what to do. You take what you can get. The tough win, losers are losers!'

'Fishbait? I wanted to thank you for showing me

how to fish and for letting me take home the fish I caught. Mum cooked it in foil in the oven. It was delicious. But just forget it. You're not nice at all.'

For the rest of the morning Adam ignored Sylvia. Nothing was said about another desk, and Adam decided not to make a big deal about it. Sylvia was strangely quiet and kept to herself. Maybe she's thinking about what I said, Adam thought.

While they were writing answers on a short piece of writing the teacher had read to them, Adam noticed Sylvia trying to look at his work.

'Which question are you up to?' he asked.

'The first one, Fatso.'

'Use my name, Sylvia, or I'm not going to help you.'

She paused. 'The first one, Adam.'

'Where did the children live?'

'In a cottage by the sea,' replied Sylvia.

'That's right. What's the next question?'

'You read it to me.'

'No,' Adam told her. He waited. She looked at the whiteboard but said nothing.

'How did the children help their mother?' he finally asked.

'They made toys to sell at the market.'

'You know the answers to the questions, so you must have listened to Ms Smith reading. Do you have trouble reading, Sylvia?'

'No.' She glared at Adam. She looked away and then she looked right in his eyes. 'Sometimes. Maybe I have a bit of trouble.'

'I'll make a deal with you. I'll help you in class, if you stop being a bully... and if you keep teaching me how to fish.'

'It's a deal, Fishbait. I mean, Adam. See you at the river after school.'

'See you then, Fishergirl.'

Activities and Discussion

Friendly or Unfriendly Behaviour

After a class discussion about friendly and unfriendly behaviours, ask the students to move into small groups.

Present each group with a copy of the activity sheet Identifying Negative and Positive Behaviours.

Ask the students to list, under the heading 'Unfriendly and Negative Behaviours', the types of negative behaviours or situations that could promote or be classed as bullying in a school environment. For example:

- inequality in playground space
- gender or age issues
- inadequate sports equipment
- trouble spots in the playground
- not being invited to join in a game
- pushing in the canteen line
- name-calling
- hitting or punching.

Ask the students to also list, under the heading 'Friendly and Positive Behaviours', what could take place in a school to help students feel safe, and promote a sense of belonging. For example:

- asking someone to join in a game
- sharing equipment with another
- waiting patiently for a turn at something
- accepting differences in race, religion, sex or disability.

Each group then reports their findings to the class. These may be documented by the teacher on a sheet of A3 paper or board for future reference.

Scenarios

Each group may then choose a scenario from the list of unfriendly and friendly behaviours (already identified by the students in the previous activity) to role-play to the whole class.

As each group concludes its role-play, ask the class to identify the negative behaviours and brainstorm possible solutions for a more positive outcome.

If time allows, invite some groups to repeat their scenario to the class. This time, however, the role-play should include both the original scenario and the scenario depicting the solution.

It is important to emphasise to the students that there are guidelines to determine acceptable and unacceptable behaviour when role-playing. The teacher should monitor the group activity closely to ensure that students do not misuse the role-playing exercise.

The Scenarios activity sheet can be used to record the groups' win-lose scenario and to promote discussion on more positive outcomes.

Feeling Valued

Give each student a copy of the activity sheet Feeling Valued. This activity will promote friendliness, and assist students to feel valued and recognised for their special gifts, talents or differences.

Emphasise that everyone has a special gift or talent and positive qualities. Ask the students to list the students in your class under the heading 'Names'. Next to each name, write keywords that describe what that person is good at, and a positive quality or value that person has, for example, Kym is good at sport and is a kind person. They cannot use the same adjective (for example, 'nice') more than three times. Ask the students to think hard about each person: they shouldn't ask them or others but reach their own conclusions.

When the students have completed the task, ask them to cut each person's information out and hand it to the relevant student so they can stick all of the positive strips about themselves into their health book or journal.

This activity is a great reminder to students about their individual, positive talents and qualities that others observe.

Promoting Friendly Behaviour

Ask the students to design a brochure using the activity sheet Promoting Friendly Behaviour Brochure for your school. They should include examples of friendly behaviour that they think their school should reinforce.

What are the benefits of friendly behaviour and what type of learning environment do they promote?

Alternatively, they may like to design their brochure on a computer.

When completed, ask the students to present their brochures to the class then display it in their classroom.

Friendship Showbag

Ask the students to create and decorate a Friendship Showbag. Items they could make to include in their showbag are:

  ▸   a friendship bracelet (made with coloured strands of wool)

  ▸   compliment cards

  ▸   a picture that they have drawn for a friend

  ▸   small items or gimmicks that promote the concept of friendliness.

Identifying Negative and Positive Behaviours

Unfriendly and negative behaviours at school

_____

_____

_____

_____

_____

_____

_____

_____

_____

_____

Friendly and positive behaviours at school

_____

_____

_____

_____

_____

_____

_____

_____

_____

_____

Scenarios

Win-Lose Scenario

Unfriendly behaviour

Win-Win Scenario

Realistic solutions for a more positive outcome

Feeling Valued

List the names of your class. Beside each name, write keywords that describe what that person is good at and a positive quality or value that person displays.

Name	Special talent and positive quality

Promoting Friendly Behaviour Brochure

Design a brochure promoting friendly behaviour for your school.

Objectives

▸ To help students identify major values they consider when deciding right from wrong behaviour.

▸ To help students identify major influences on behaviour.

▸ To help students examine the importance of honesty.

Factors Enhancing Resilience

▸ Promoting a sense of belonging and fitting in.

▸ Promoting proactive problem-solving.

▸ Enhancing a positive social orientation.

Introduction to the Focus Value

Brainstorm with the students and create a class definition of the focus value, 'honesty'. The students may like to use a dictionary or thesaurus to assist in defining the meaning.

With the whole class, or in small groups, discuss how honesty could be positively demonstrated in the classroom and the playground, and how they would know if it was not.

The Story: The Biggest Whopper

The story may be read by the class teacher, or in small groups if multiple copies have been made.

Follow the story with a class discussion. Some suggested questions are:

▸ What were some of the decisions faced by CJ and Kye in the story?

▸ How did CJ decide what was right and what was wrong?

▸ Do you think the boys were influenced by their consciences, by the fear of getting caught, or both? Explain.

▸ Do you think the children in the story showed different values in relation to other people's property and respect for the law? What makes you think this?

▸ Describe some strategies for responding to situations that are potentially risky or harmful.

▸ How was honesty demonstrated by the characters in the story?

Materials

▸ Decisions, Decisions activity sheet.

▸ Decision Making activity sheet.

▸ The Ripple Effect activity sheet.

▸ My Honesty Policy activity sheet.

▸ Coloured pens.

The Biggest Whopper

Written by Helen Silvester
Illustrated by Katie Jardine

Chapter 1

I used to lie. Yes, I lied every chance I got. I was really good at it too. There were very few times I couldn't get out of trouble using a good story. Most of the time, people would believe me too. That was until…

We were kicking the footy around on the way back to class after lunch, when I sneezed. The ball caught my foot at the wrong angle, went over the fence and hit an old purple car, adding to its dents. Sarah and Kye kept watch as I jumped over the fence to grab the ball from the gutter. All of a sudden, a lady appeared from the other side of the car. She was sort of pretty, in a gypsy kind of way. She almost rattled with all the beads around her neck. Quick as anything, a lie came to me – you know, one of those lies that are always there in case of emergency.

'Wish I had seen who kicked it, Miss, but he ran off too quickly.' I turned and winked at the others and started back over the fence.

'You lie often, do you not?' The lady sounded really old-fashioned, even though she was nowhere near as old as my mother. Her eyes were strange: very green and staring.

I decided she wasn't a threat.

'Not too often.' I threw the ball to Kye and Sarah and jumped after it.

'Young man.'

The bell started ringing, but her voice stopped me. Kye and Sarah kept running as I looked over my shoulder. She stood there, pointing at me.

'Be it as you say.' She didn't shout it, but it still sounded like a warning.

'Come on CJ. We'll be late again,' yelled Sarah, disappearing around the corner.

Chapter 2

I had forgotten all about the football by the time I was back in the classroom. Mrs Stripe was already there. Everyone was pulling out grammar books to check their homework. Papers flew everywhere as I grabbed my book out of my bag. Mrs Stripe came over almost immediately. She was always on my back about finishing work, being on time and doing homework. All those things teachers think are important.

'I suppose your homework is in amongst those scattered papers, CJ?'

Of course it wasn't, because I hadn't done it, as usual. Quickly, I grabbed one of the ripped sheets of paper from the floor and held it out to Mrs Stripe.

'No, Mrs Stripe. I did finish it, but you wouldn't believe me if I told you what happened to it.'

'Try me, CJ.'

'Well, I left it on the table last night before I went to bed. It must have fallen onto the floor next to Boris. He's our dog. Well, he must have eaten it because this morning all I found was this corner still covered in his slobber. See, I told you that you wouldn't believe me.'

Mrs Stripe blinked in disbelief. 'You're telling me your dog ate it?'

I nodded.

'OK then.' She thought for a moment. 'If you really did complete it last night, then it won't take you long to do it again after school this afternoon.'

What could I do but nod my head? I had arranged to go to Kye's that afternoon to plan his birthday party next week.

The rest of the lesson went slowly, as Mrs Stripe's lessons always did. She didn't let up on me for a minute. As soon as the bell rang, I grabbed my books to try to slip out the door, but Mrs Stripe was already there.

'CJ,' she said warningly.

Cornered, I headed back to my desk.

'Excuse me, Mrs Stripe?'

Turning, I saw my mum at the door. 'Could I see you for a moment?'

Mrs Stripe spoke to my mum at the door for a few minutes. Mum had a strange, worried look on her face.

'I owe you an apology, CJ,' said Mrs Stripe, beckoning me over. 'Your mother has just told me about Boris. I hope he is all right. I'll see you tomorrow.'

Mum started to hurry me towards the car. 'Come on,' she said. 'They should have finished the operation by now. I hope they got out all that paper of yours.'

'What paper? What happened?'

'Your rotten homework. How many times have I told you to put it away when you've finished. Boris would never have eaten it if you had put it in your bag like I told you to.'

The lie I had told came back to me. It had been just a story, hadn't it? It couldn't be true.

But it was. At the vet's, Boris was lying asleep in a cage. At least, he looked like he was just asleep, but there were ugly stitches in his side. The vet said Boris would probably be okay, but that he wouldn't know for sure until the next day.

Chapter 3

The trip home was quiet. We were worried about Boris. As we drove into the garage, I remembered that I was supposed to go to Kye's after school to plan his party. As soon as the car was switched off I said, 'I promised Kye I would go to his place this afternoon to help him with his homework. Is it still all right if I go?'

Mum quickly looked over. She had caught me out in a few of my stories recently and was beginning to doubt some of the things I said. I hoped my lie sounded plausible.

'OK,' she said carefully. 'But remember to be back by six.'

I grinned and grabbed my bag out of the car.

Kye's mum answered the door and told me Kye was in the living room. Kye looked up with relief when he heard me. Books surrounded him, and sheets of paper were scattered all over the table.

'Have you done question four yet? I just can't work it out.'

'What question four?' I asked.

'Question four on the English assignment. It's due tomorrow.'

'What assignment? We weren't given an assignment in English.'

'Yes we were. Right after we corrected the grammar homework.' Kye held up a sheet of paper covered in questions. It looked like one of Mrs Stripe's sheets, but I had never seen this one before. The date at the top said it was due the next day. I grabbed my grammar book out of my bag and, sure enough, a similar sheet was tucked in the front of it.

'You promised me you would help me with it,' Kye reminded me.

This was getting weird; I had come over to plan his birthday party. The only time I had even thought about homework was when I had told Mum that Kye needed my help. What could I do? Sighing, I sat down and opened my grammar book to a fresh page. The party would have to wait. I couldn't use the 'dog ate my homework' excuse again.

Chapter 4

Mum didn't believe me when I was late for dinner that night, until I showed her the homework that Kye and I had only just finished.

In the morning, I was up early to plan the footy team for that weekend. I was the captain, and each week I had to present the list to Mr Heard, the coach, before it was put up on the notice board. It took me an hour to finish.

At breakfast, Mum asked me about my room and, as usual, I said I had already tidied it. This time, however, she went to check. I waited for the usual lecture about my room being my responsibility. Instead, she said, 'Well done CJ. You must have spent an hour cleaning up. I couldn't have done better. I'm sorry I doubted you.'

'But…' Quickly, I swallowed the rest of my toast and went back to my room. It was spotless. Everything was in its right place, and the floor even looked as though it had been vacuumed. I knew I hadn't done it, and yet it was clean.

'Come on, CJ. Time to go!' Mum yelled from the kitchen.

Resolving to get to the bottom of the mystery later, I grabbed my bag and ran out to the car.

Mr Heard was on playground duty when Mum dropped me at the school gate.

'Have you got the team list for me to check, CJ?' he asked as I went past.

'Yeah. I did it this morning.' I said, hunting through my bag for the list I had made before breakfast. It wasn't in the side pocket where I thought I had put it. It wasn't in the centre of my bag either.

'Come on, CJ. Don't tell me one of your stories again. If you haven't done it, just say so.'

'But I have done it. I made the list out this morning before breakfast.'

'CJ, if you're lying again, I'll have to replace you as captain. It's a position of responsibility and I can't have the captain of our team lying to cover up laziness.'

'But I'm not lying. I did write down the team this morning.' I tipped all of my books on the ground in frustration. Papers blew the length of the school fence.

'CJ, that's it! You're no longer team captain. Pick up those papers and I'll see you at practice this afternoon. That is, if you're still in the team. Leave your lies behind this time.' Mr Heard turned and walked off.

I felt my eyes prickle. Frustrated, I gathered up the scattered papers, not caring how crushed they were. Things had been going wrong ever since yesterday. First Boris had got sick, then Kye had wanted to do homework instead of planning his party, and then the team list had disappeared as if I had never done it. The only good thing that had happened was that my room had cleaned itself. I stopped for a minute and went through it all again slowly. First, I had told Mrs Stripe that Boris had eaten my homework, and he had. Then I told Mum that Kye needed help with his homework, and he did. Now the footy list had disappeared as if I had really spent an hour tidying my room and not worked out the team list at all. Three lies had come true. Slowly, I swung my bag onto my back. This needed some more thought. The bell rang and I ran to class, trying to think of how I could control the next lie.

Chapter 5

That morning went well. For once, I didn't have to lie about my homework, as I had done it with Kye the night before. To test my theory, I deliberately didn't put in my lunch order. When the lunches were passed out, Mrs Stripe noticed that I didn't have anything to eat.

'Did you bring your lunch today, CJ?'

'No, Mrs Stripe. I ordered one.' Carefully I looked around the room. Everyone was checking their bags. I pointed to Sarah. She always ordered a large lunch with lots of junk food.

'That one's mine.'

Sarah looked up, surprised. Mrs Stripe asked, 'Is that yours Sarah, or is it CJ's?'

Puzzled, Sarah checked the name on the bag. Mrs Stripe went over to look too. My name was now on the bag in big black letters.

'It's yours, CJ.' Mrs Stripe picked up the bag and gave it to me.

'Did you order your lunch Sarah, or do you need to get a Marmite sandwich from the office freezer?'

The sandwiches in the office freezer were for those students who forgot their lunches. They were frozen hard and always dry and stale. They usually ensured that everyone remembered his or her lunch.

Feeling guilty, I said to Sarah, 'How about we share the lunch?'

Sarah wore the same bewildered expression that I must have worn several times since the day before.

'I was sure I put my lunch order in this morning.'

'Don't worry. There's enough for both of us.'

As we ate our lunch, I thought about the possibilities. Four times now my lies had come true. I would have to be careful about how I said things to make sure nothing bad happened. It seemed that I could say almost anything and it would be true. I could say I had a particular CD or video, even a Game Boy, and it would be true. I could even become a champion football player. Coach would have to make me captain again.

After lunch, I suggested to Kye and Sarah that we go to the corner of the playground where we usually hung out. I had decided to enlist their help in the next lie.

As we passed the office, Mr Heard saw me and called me over. Next to him was the gypsy lady from the day before. The beads still jingled around her neck.

I'll need to be careful, I thought.

'CJ, Ms Fide asked if I could locate the person who kicked the ball into her car yesterday. She said you were there and might have seen what happened. Did you?'

'Me? I was there, but I didn't see who kicked the ball.' That was at least true. Sneezing had meant I shut my eyes as the ball connected with my foot.

'Are you sure?' Mr Heard persisted.

'Yes,' I said, trying to sound truthful.

'You would not lie, would you child?' Despite being quiet, the lady's voice still caught my attention. This lady was giving me the creeps.

'Me? No, Miss. I never lie.'

I never lie!

There it was – the biggest lie I had ever told, and the last. No lying to get a CD, video, or Game Boy now. No more stories to get out of homework or cleaning my room. It'll be a while before anyone believes me, but you believe me don't you? You believe my story? The lies did come true.

You know it has to be true. You see, I never lie.

Activities and Discussions

Class Discussion

Introduce the topic to students by suggesting that there are many situations in life that require us to be honest and make decisions about right and wrong behaviour.

Ask the students to give examples of these types of situations in their life, for example:

▶ Seeing friends steal something from a shop and deciding whether or not to tell the appropriate authorities.

▶ Watching a friend abuse another student with a disability and deciding whether or not to interfere.

▶ Finding money and deciding whether or not to hand it into the authorities.

▶ Catching the bus without paying for a ticket and hoping that you will not be caught.

Ask the students to discuss:

▶ How do we decide what is right and what is wrong behaviour?

▶ Which behaviours would we categorise as responsible and which as irresponsible? Identify how other people can influence your decisions to be responsible or irresponsible, honest or dishonest.

Ask the students to complete the activity sheet Decisions, Decisions.

Important Decisions

Introduce the topic by discussing the focus question:

What makes a decision good or bad?

Ask the students to move into small groups for cooperative group discussion. Ask each group to discuss what's involved in making a good, as opposed to a bad, decision.

Suggestions could include the following concepts:

▶ short-term consequences

▶ long-term consequences

▶ effects on other people

▶ effects on self

▶ time considerations

▶ money and resources

▶ potential possibilities.

Following the discussions, ask each group to identify six key factors that they considered when making their decisions. Ask them to then present these to the class for review.

The teacher may wish to list the students' suggestions on the board for display.

Using the Decision Making activity sheet, ask each student to create and design their own decision making form, drawing six important factors for consideration from the class discussion. The teacher may like to give students a model form that they can use as an example.

Using a situation from the story, fill in your form assuming the identity of one of the characters from the story.

Once the forms are completed, students can display and explain the forms they have created, and their chosen scenario from the story.

The Ripple Effect

Introduce the topic by saying that the decisions we make can have an effect on other people in our lives. Imagine that the people who are close to you are living in a pond with you.

If you liken yourself to a frog jumping off a rock and into the middle of the pond each time you make a decision, you can then see how people around you could be affected by your decision. It is called the ripple effect. Those closest to you will be affected the most by your decisions, those farthest away, the least.

Some of the decisions we make affect other people positively, like when we decide to be in a good mood and be friendly towards other family members. Some decisions affect other people negatively, like when we are in a bad mood and are nasty to others in our family.

In small groups, ask the students to discuss the following:

- How is behaviour like a ripple in the water?
- Do we have any control over the ripples we send out to others?
- Are there some things we can do to control the ripples we send out to others?
- Share a time that you helped someone else have a better day by sending out a positive ripple.

Upon conclusion of group discussion, ask each student to complete the activity sheet The Ripple Effect.

My Honesty Policy

Ask the students to work individually or in small groups and complete the activity sheet My Honesty Policy. The concept of honesty and tact can be discussed.

Decisions, Decisions

Think about an important decision you had to make. If you can't think of one, imagine one instead. What was the decision? In the space provided below, write about the long and short-term consequences of your decision.

Win-Lose Situation or Bad Decision (e.g. not being honest)

_____

_____

Short-term consequence

_____

_____

Long-term consequence

_____

_____

List some key factors you considered when making your decision

_____

_____

_____

_____

Win-Win Situation or Good Decision (e.g. telling the truth)

_____

_____

Short-term consequence

_____

_____

Long-term consequence

_____

_____

List some key factors you considered when making your decision

_____

_____

_____

_____

Decision Making

Create and design your own decision making form. Identify and list six key factors to consider when making an important decision in your life.

The Ripple Effect

Think about one positive action and one negative action of yours that has had an effect on someone else. It may be to do with being honest or dishonest. Write these in the 'My Action' circle on the diagram below.

Positive Ripples

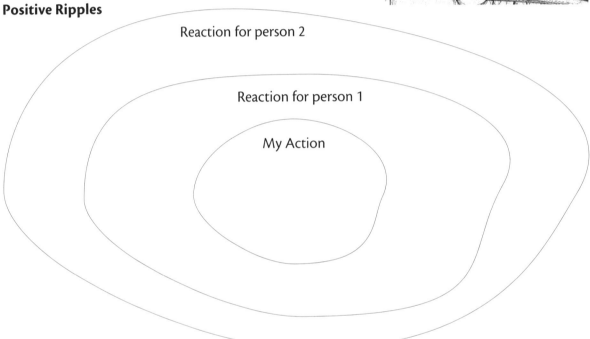

Reaction for person 2

Reaction for person 1

My Action

Negative Ripples

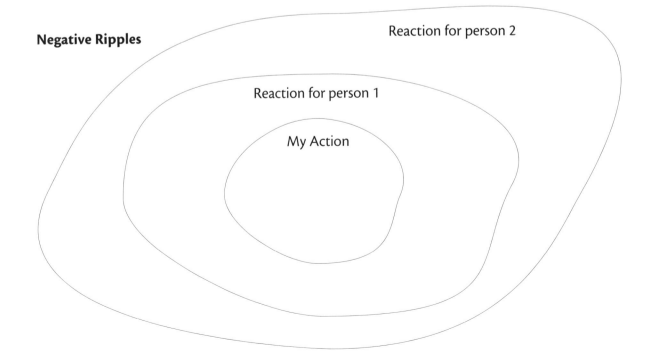

Reaction for person 2

Reaction for person 1

My Action

My Honesty Policy

'Honesty is the best policy'

Explain what you think this statement means.

What does the word 'tact' mean? (You may like to use a dictionary.)

Honesty sometimes requires people to be tactful. Explain.

In the space below, create your own policy for Honesty.
(You may like to include the concept of being tactful.)

My Honesty Policy

On the back of this sheet, design a cartoon strip demonstrating your Honesty Policy.

Objectives

▸ To assist students to examine the way stereotypes are presented in the community.

▸ To help students identify the disadvantages of defining people in terms of a stereotype.

▸ To help students examine the way health information and services can be accessed and used to assist the promotion of wellbeing and good health.

▸ To help students examine the importance of kindness.

Factors Enhancing Resilience

▸ Promoting proactive problem-solving.

▸ Enhancing positive social orientation.

▸ Encouraging an optimistic sense of future.

▸ Recognising a special talent.

▸ Promoting a sense of belonging and fitting in.

Introduction to the Focus Value

Brainstorm with the students and create a class definition of the focus value, 'kindness'. The students may like to use a dictionary or thesaurus to assist in defining the meaning.

With the whole class, or in small groups, discuss how the kindness could be positively demonstrated in the classroom and the playground, and how they would know if it was not.

The Story: Sophie's Gift

The story may be read to the students by the teacher, or in small groups if multiple copies have been made.

Follow the story with a class discussion. Some suggested questions are:

▸ In the story Sophie's Gift, two very different lifestyles were presented. What were they? For example, wealthy, opulent, homeless or poverty stricken.

▸ What scenes and descriptions in the story lead you to your conclusions?

▸ Do you think Sophie's behaviour and reaction toward Jack and his family situation was appropriate? Why?

▸ Why do you think some young people end up being homeless? Is it necessarily their fault?

▸ What are some disadvantages in stereotyping people?

▸ Do you think that Sophie's reaction to give chase was a sensible one? Why? What could have been dangerous about the situation?

▸ If you were in Sophie's shoes, would you have chased the young male to get back your jacket?

▸ In what ways did Sophie help Jack?

▸ What other people or organisations are there in your community who help young people in need?

Materials

- ▸ Making Assumptions activity sheet.
- ▸ Magazines and newspapers.
- ▸ Making a Difference activity sheet.
- ▸ Stereotypes activity sheet.
- ▸ Acts of Kindness activity sheet.

Sophie's Gift

Written by Michael Dell
Illustrated by Lori Head

Chapter 1

'What do you want for Christmas, Sophie?' asked her uncle, beaming down on her where she sat reading the latest issue of her favourite equestrian magazine.

'I'm not sure, Uncle Ted,' she replied.

He frowned. 'Surely there's something you need. How about some new clothes?'

'That would be nice,' replied Sophie, trying to concentrate on her magazine.

'You're too good to her, Ted. I only wish she would show more appreciation,' said Sophie's mum.

'Perhaps she would show more appreciation for the good things in life if she'd had our upbringing,' put in Sophie's dad.

'I'm sure she would,' agreed her mum. 'Now say thank you to Uncle Ted, Sophie.'

'Thank you Uncle Ted,' said Sophie obediently.

'You're most welcome, Princess,' said her uncle smiling.

'I'm going to read in my room, Mum,' said Sophie.

'Well, don't be long. Uncle Ted wants to leave shortly,' said Mum.

Sophie lay on her bed, no longer able to concentrate on the magazine. She contemplated the luxury of her room.

Her white dressing table held an array of expensive dolls, and a partly open door led to a walk-in wardrobe filled with clothes bearing designer labels. The bed she lay on was covered in a snow-white quilt decorated with small, pink roses. When she stood to cross to the window, her feet sank into the luxury of deep pile carpet.

She watched from the window as her horse, Star, cropped the sweet grass in his paddock with the setting sun making a glorious backdrop to the scene.

Sophie had everything most girls dreamed of, but she was not happy. Maybe if she had a brother or sister she would be more content, but her parents appeared happy with the family the way it was.

Uncle Ted was Mum's brother, and among his many business interests was the stud farm where Sophie lived with her parents. Dad managed the place for him while Mum kept the accounts.

Uncle Ted had no children of his own, so he lavished money and affection on Sophie. He even paid the fees for the expensive school she attended. The purpose of that day's visit was to go over recent business with Sophie's parents, then take her into the city to see the Christmas decorations.

Sophie sighed as she changed into jeans and runners. She really did not feel like going out tonight, but felt she should show some appreciation as her parents had suggested. She put on her new, soft, leather jacket and left the room to join her uncle.

Chapter 2

The city was crowded with Christmas shoppers and the decorations were magnificent.

Sophie's dark mood lifted as she heard the sweet voices of a children's choir singing carols in the city square. A warm breeze was blowing, so she took off her jacket and swung it over her shoulder.

'Hey, Ted!' called a man, pushing his way through the crowd to greet her uncle.

'Ernie! Merry Christmas,' said her uncle.

The two men moved to a shop doorway where they immediately began to discuss business.

After listening to five minutes of boring shoptalk, Sophie politely interrupted their conversation.

'Would it be all right if I go to get a drink?' she asked.

'Okay Princess, but don't wander off. Anyway, I believe I forgot my manners. Ernie, this is my niece. Sophie, I would like you to meet a business friend of mine, Ernie Bates,' replied her uncle.

Sophie smiled at Ernie who nodded briefly in her direction before turning back to his conversation with her uncle. He was obviously irritated at having been interrupted. What a rude man, thought Sophie.

She moved to a nearby kiosk where she ordered a can of soft drink. Placing her jacket on the counter, she took the money from the pocket of her jeans to pay for the drink.

Suddenly, a hand moved in front of her and snatched the jacket from the counter, leaving her open mouthed with shock. She turned her head to see a group of youths weaving their way through the crowd with an expertise obviously born of long practice.

Sophie started to chase them, but soon realised she was wasting her time as they got further away. About to give up the chase Sophie noticed a distinctive red baseball cap among the group peel off and dart into a shopping centre. Taking up the chase again, she soon lost him among the mass of Christmas shoppers.

Dejectedly, Sophie sat on a bench to catch her breath while she scanned the passing faces for a sign of the youths. Her gaze finally rested on a red cap only two benches away from where she sat.

The youth was breathing hard as she sidled over, being careful not to cause alarm and make him flee again.

'Gotcha,' she said, gripping him firmly by the arm.

'Oh no!' groaned the boy, removing his hat and wiping it across his sweaty face.

'Not a very competent thief are you?' said Sophie.

'Hey, I'm no thief,' answered the boy hotly.

'Yeah, right. Give me my jacket back or I'll call that police officer,' said Sophie, indicating a passing officer.

'I haven't got your rotten jacket,' said the boy. His shoulders slumped in despair.

'Look,' he continued, 'I only met those kids an hour ago. They said they were going to show me a place I could sleep tonight. How was I to know they were going to steal your jacket?'

Sophie took in the boy's look of defeat as he sat hunched on the bench.

Finally, she said, 'Maybe I'm making a big mistake, but I think you're telling the truth. What's your name?'

'Jack,' he mumbled.

Sophie offered him her hand to shake.

'Hello Jack, I'm Sophie. Now, what are you doing looking for somewhere to sleep when you should be at home? You're only a kid.'

'It's a long story,' answered Jack. 'I've been living rough for about two weeks now.'

'Are you hungry?' asked Sophie. Jack nodded his head.

'Come on, let's get a burger. Then you can help me to get my jacket back.'

Jack swallowed the last of his burger and finished his drink. He sighed contentedly and settled back in his chair.

'That was great,' he said.

'Okay, now for my jacket,' said Sophie.

'I already told you, Sophie, I don't know those kids.'

'But you must have some idea where they hang out. That jacket was an expensive present from my uncle and I want it back,' demanded Sophie.

'Oh you poor thing. It must be so awful to have your nice jacket taken from you,' replied Jack, his voice heavy with sarcasm.

'What gives you the right to speak to me like that?' said Sophie. 'Okay, so you think I'm rich, but that doesn't give anyone the right to take things just because they want them.'

'Maybe they needed the jacket. Do you know what it's like living the way they do?' fumed Jack.

'I don't care how bad things are, they still don't have the right to steal,' said Sophie, matching his anger with her own.

Jack's eyes suddenly widened in alarm. 'Oh no! I have to go,' he said.

Sophie followed his gaze to the police officer who was making his way towards them in the company of an anxious looking Uncle Ted.

'Stay there,' she said as Jack rose from the table.

'Not me. I'm off,' he replied, tipping his chair over in his haste to escape. Sophie hung on to his jumper, restraining him.

'No you don't, son, I want to talk to you,' said the officer, grabbing Jack's arm.

'Let me go. I haven't done anything,' pleaded Jack, trying to break the officer's grip.

'Sophie! Where have you been? I've been searching for you for over an hour,' said Uncle Ted in obvious distress.

'You traitor!' shouted Jack as the police officer led him away.

'Where is he taking him?' cried Sophie.

'To the police station, probably.'

'But why? He hasn't done anything.'

'I suppose the police officer recognised him as a minor in need of help,' said Uncle Ted. 'Come on, love. Let's get you home.'

'No, I want to go to the police station to find out what's going to happen to Jack,' said Sophie firmly.

Chapter 3

'This is Miss Barrett,' said the sergeant, introducing a young woman dressed in T-shirt and jeans to Sophie and Uncle Ted.

'Call me Joan,' she said, taking a seat opposite them in the interview room. 'I'm a social worker. I do what I can to help some of the homeless kids.'

'Only some of them?' queried Sophie.

'Those that want to be helped,' answered Joan.

'I don't think we understand,' said Uncle Ted.

'Then let me explain. You see, there are children who are genuinely homeless due to circumstances I won't go into at present. It's those cases that need the most help. Then there are others who leave home by choice, mostly to avoid parental control. They see street life as an exciting alternative. Many of them soon come to realise the grim reality and return home by choice. Unfortunately, there are others who get

caught in a downward spiral of drugs and despair. They are the really hard ones to help.'

'And what category does young Jack fall into?' asked Uncle Ted.

'Jack is an unusual case,' said Joan. 'His mother lost the family home recently, and Jack thought that by leaving home he would ease the burden on her. He could not have been more wrong. He caused his mother even more grief by disappearing the way he did.'

'What will happen to him now?' asked Sophie.

'We've located his mother. She's living in temporary accommodation. I'll be returning Jack to his family, which should be a great relief to them all,' said Joan.

Chapter 4

'Well, all's well that ends well,' said Uncle Ted. 'Come on, Sophie. Let's get you home.'

The lights of the city gave way to the quieter country roads as Sophie made her way home with Uncle Ted.

'Cheer up, Princess. It'll be Christmas soon,' he said in an effort to lighten her obviously gloomy mood.

'I'm sorry, I just can't stop thinking about Jack and all those other kids,' said Sophie.

'I know. It's a sad situation, Sophie, but we can't shoulder all the world's problems,' he replied.

They drove on in silence for a time before Sophie spoke again.

'I've decided what I want for Christmas, Uncle Ted,' she said.

He looked over at her with his eyebrows raised quizzically.

'I'd like you to use the money you were going to spend on me, to give Jack's family a decent Christmas,' she said.

'Oh Sophie, one good Christmas isn't going to change their lives,' he said.

'I know, Uncle Ted, but it's a start. And we could think more about helping people less fortunate than ourselves from now on,' she went on enthusiastically.

'Oh, come on Sophie, we all have our problems, you know.'

'Our problems are nothing compared with those of families like Jack's. Anyway, suppose everyone thought that way. There would be nobody like Joan Barrett to care for others.'

'All right,' said Uncle Ted resignedly. 'But we don't even know where Jack and his family are living.'

'Call Joan Barrett. I'm sure she could help,' said Sophie.

Her uncle smiled at her with a shake of his head. 'You really are a determined young lady,' he said.

Chapter 5

After their ride Sophie led Star into his stall and began rubbing him down. As she worked, she wondered how Jack and his family were coping. Christmas was long over and Uncle Ted had been as good as his word in providing food and toys to the struggling family.

'There's someone here to see you,' called Mum from the house.

Sophie was surprised and delighted to find Joan Barrett drinking a cup of tea in the kitchen.

'Hi Sophie. I had to make a trip out this way so I thought I'd drop in and give you an update on Jack,' she said.

It was a good report. Jack was back in school and doing well. His mother had a new job and the family had recently moved into permanent accommodation. Sophie was thrilled.

'Your uncle has been of tremendous help,' said Joan.

'Really?' said Sophie, surprised.

'Yes. He seems to have taken a new interest in helping disadvantaged families. Oh, by the way, I have something for you from Jack's mum.'

Joan handed Sophie a card. She opened it and read the message written inside. 'Thank you.'

'That message conveys more than the simple words on the card, Sophie,' said Joan. 'If it weren't for you and your concern for Jack, his family would have spent a miserable Christmas not knowing if he was safe. Now, through you and your uncle's generosity, Jack's family has been given hope. It just shows that one person can make a difference.'

Activities and Discussion

Making Assumptions

Introduce the topic by saying that sometimes we make snap decisions or assumptions about people before we get to know them.

Using magazines or newspapers, ask small groups of students to cut out a picture of a person with a striking facial expression. They should paste the picture onto the activity sheet Making Assumptions.

Underneath the picture, ask the students to write some statistics and general information about the person from the article.

Using another piece of paper, ask them to make a flap that covers the writing. Ask each group to talk or write about another group's character without looking at the information under the flap. They should notice the assumptions they make about the person, just by looking at them. The groups can then report their findings to the class.

Suggest to the class that sometimes our judgments are harsh and unkind.

Discuss the idea of 'giving people the benefit of the doubt'.

What does it mean in terms of 'kindness'?

Making a Difference

Introduce the topic by saying that in the story, Sophie was kind and helped Jack in a number of ways. She made a real difference to him and to the lives of those in his family.

Ask the students to discuss the following in small groups:

If you chose to make a difference in the world, what area would it be in?

Ask them to then report their findings back to the class.

The class teacher could list the student suggestions on the board. Some suggestions could include:

- ▸ homeless people
- ▸ the elderly
- ▸ wildlife
- ▸ the environment
- ▸ starving children in other countries
- ▸ providing free medical assistance and education programmes to those in need; creating a teenage drop-in centre
- ▸ helping ethnic groups.

Ask the students to choose an area that they feel strongly or passionately about.

Ask the students to think what their vision would look like, if they had access to unlimited funds to create an organisation that helped in their area of interest:

- ▸ What would you do?
- ▸ How would you organise it?
- ▸ What would your main aim be?

Follow up with the activity sheet Making a Difference.

Stereotypes

Have a class discussion and consider what the term 'stereotype' means (for example, label, tag, categorise or pigeonhole).

Ask the students to list some of the negative aspects of stereotyping people. Ask them to brainstorm some common stereotypes used by people. Are there some common characteristics that people in certain groups have? (For example, military people.)

Using the activity sheet Stereotypes, ask the students to draw their impression of a common stereotype of one of the following:

- ▶ a military person
- ▶ an artist
- ▶ an athlete
- ▶ a politician
- ▶ a teacher.

Ask the students to create a stereotype of a kind person. They should think about what a 'kind' person would look like to them, including facial expressions, gender, age and so on.

Acts of Kindness

As a small group or whole class, ask the students to discuss an act of kindness that they could perform as a class that would help the school in a positive way. For example:

- ▶ creating a special environmental garden
- ▶ cleaning up a specific area that needs beautifying
- ▶ helping teachers and/or other students in some way.

Ask the students to:

- ▶ Create a taskforce to implement your 'act of kindness'.
- ▶ Plan a timeline and a list of the materials that you will require to complete you chosen activity.
- ▶ Allocate specific tasks.
- ▶ Implement your planned 'Act of Kindness'. Remember to seek permission from the headteacher to undertake the task if the class teacher deems it necessary to do so.

Using the activity sheet Acts of Kindness, let individuals specify what they could do to be kinder at home, school and in the community.

Making Assumptions

Using magazines or newspapers cut out a picture of a person with a striking facial expression. Paste the picture in the box.

My impressions and information about the person in the picture:

1. ....

2. ....

3. ....

4. ....

5. ....

6. ....

7. ....

Making a Difference

In the box below, design a business card or pamphlet that describes your organisation and what it stands for. (You may wish to use a computer programme for this.)

If you are designing a business card, show both sides of the card. Include a logo and catchy phrase for promotion.

Present your business card or pamphlet to the class.

The business cards and pamphlets can make a great display in the classroom.

Front of Business Card

Back of Business Card

Stereotypes

Draw your impression of your chosen common stereotype
then draw your impression of a kind person.

A common stereotype.

My stereotype of a kind person.

Acts of Kindness

Write about or draw what you could do to be kinder:

At home

At school

In the community

Objectives

▸ To assist students to identify major influences on health.

▸ To help students identify physical, social and emotional changes that are common to both sexes during puberty.

▸ To assist student awareness of the importance of personal hygiene.

▸ To help students examine the importance of responsibility.

Factors Enhancing Resilience

▸ Promoting a sense of belonging and fitting in.

▸ Promoting proactive problem-solving.

▸ Enhancing a positive social orientation.

Introduction to the Focus Value

Brainstorm with the students and create a class definition of the focus value, 'responsibility'. The students may like to use a dictionary or thesaurus to assist in defining the meaning.

With the whole class, or in small groups, discuss how the value of responsibility could be positively demonstrated in the classroom and the playground, and how they would know if it was not.

The Story: Stinky Josh

The story may be read to the class by the teacher, or in small groups if multiple copies have been made.

Follow the story with a class discussion. Some suggested questions are:

In what ways did the characters in the story demonstrate responsibility?

▸ When Josh returned to the classroom, what did he do that Mr Valconi was not happy about?

▸ Why were Amy, Mario and Sophie all unhappy with Josh?

▸ Do you think Amy did the right thing when she was so honest with Josh?

▸ When Josh spoke to Tim in the reading corner, did Tim give him good advice?

▸ What was Josh's attitude to his personal hygiene? What changes did he decide to make? Why?

▸ Do you agree with Josh's mum when she says that we're all judged by the way we look? How important is personal appearance? How can we make the best of our appearance?

▸ When Josh cleaned the mouse cage, he showed that he could be thoughtful and clean. Why is it important to clean up after pets and provide them with a clean area to live in?

Materials

▸ Images of Health activity sheet.

▸ Magazines, glue and coloured pens.

▸ Growing Up activity sheet.

▸ Creating Wellbeing activity sheet.

▸ My Helpful Services List activity sheet.

Stinky Josh

Written by Leanne Winfield
Illustrated by Katie Jardine

Chapter 1

It was lunch-time at school. Josh was sitting on a bench outside the canteen, eating a sausage roll.

'Let's play a game,' Tim suggested.

'Yep. I'll just finish eating.'

'Ugh, Josh! You've just slopped sauce all down your jumper! Uck, what a mess!'

'Umm, never mind,' Josh said, trying to wipe it off with the paper bag.

'You're making it worse. Go to the drinking taps and wash it off.'

'No. It'll be all wet then. Who cares about a bit of tomato sauce? Come on, let's go play.'

When the bell went at the end of lunch-time, Josh and Tim returned to their classroom.

'You look like you've been in the wars,' said Josh's teacher, Mr Valconi, noticing the blood-like stain on Josh's football jumper. 'And you didn't worry too much about the mud either, Josh. Go and wipe your feet outside please.'

'Um, Mr Valconi, what mud?'

'That mud!' He said, pointing to the clumps Josh had trailed in. 'Just do it, please Josh.'

Josh wiped his feet on the concrete outside and returned to his seat beside Amy Lee.

'Phew, you smell, Josh,' she said. 'Did you stand in something other than mud? Have you had a shower in the last few days, or is it the week-old socks that you never take off your feet? I know, it's foot odour escaping from your holey trainers! And when did you last clean your teeth?'

'Just the smell of an athlete, Amy. Take note of it.'

'No thanks! Can you smell someone who's off, Mario? Sophie?' Amy asked the boy and girl sitting at the next desk.

'Oh. Josh, Josh have a wash,' Mario said pulling a face.

'Josh, have a wash,' Amy and Sophie joined in with Mario.

'Here, have some of my deodorant spray, Josh,' Sophie said, handing it to him.

'No way! I don't want to smell like you Amy! Although, for a girl, you do smell pretty good.'

'We'd rather you smell like a girl than like a football boot!' Mario said laughing.

'You're nagging me just like my mum does. Get a life! I'm going to sit in the reading corner to escape from the smell police.'

Chapter 2

In the reading corner, Josh tried to smell himself. He wrinkled his nose and sniffed. He smelt normal. What were they all going on about? He'd had a shower, but he couldn't quite remember when. Maybe it was a couple of days ago.

When did he last change his socks? The ones he had on did look a little bit grey. And there were holes in his trainers, but Mum had promised to buy him a new pair this weekend. He put his hand up to his mouth and breathed out, trying to smell his breath. He had cleaned his teeth that morning, he was sure of it.

'What are you doing, Josh?' Tim asked as he sat down on a chair next to Josh.

'Trying to smell myself.'

'What?'

'Never mind. What do you think Amy will say if I ask her to come with us to the football on Saturday?'

'I think she'll probably say no. Girls are a bit picky, Josh. They like tidiness. Maybe if you wore a different jumper and cleaned yourself up a bit she might say yes.'

'Um, perhaps you're right,'

Josh said as he looked at Tim who appeared as fresh as if he had just arrived at school. Some people are able to stay neat all day. How do they do that? Josh wondered.

It wasn't that Josh wanted to be dirty; it was just that he didn't think a lot about being clean. He would make some changes this weekend, beginning with reminding his mum to buy him new shoes.

Chapter 3

'Josh, come on! We're running late!' Mum yelled from down the hallway. 'Let's get you out of your old, holey shoes now that it's winter.'

'I can't find my football jumper.'

'It's probably in the pile of dirty clothes you've left at the end of your bed,' said Mum, coming up the stairs. 'Wear one of the clean ones hanging up in your wardrobe.'

'I want to wear my favourite!'

'If it's not in the wardrobe, then it's not clean. If you leave your dirty clothes here, they're never going to be washed. Look at this mess,' Mum said, looking around at the clothes, half finished puzzles and mess lying around on the floor.

'No wonder you can't find anything. This room is a health hazard. And put on clean socks please. If we're trying on runners, I don't want to be embarrassed by grubby, smelly socks.'

'Yes, I put on clean socks, after I had my shower and before I cleaned my teeth. But I can't be bothered with the clothes.'

'Neither can I. I've enough to do without sorting through your clothes as well.'

'Muuummmm… Ahh, here it is.' Josh pulled the jumper over his head.

'You can't wear that! It has a huge tomato sauce stain on it!'

'Who cares?' replied Josh.

'I do. Rightly or wrongly, everyone is judged by the way they look. And I don't mean that you have to look like a movie star, or always wear brand name clothes, but you have to be clean. As well as having a shower, you have to wear clean clothes.'

'All right. I'll wear my other brown jumper.'

'I want this room cleaned up when we get home. Those mice stink. When was the last time you cleaned their cage?' questioned his mum.

'What about Angela's room? You never go off at her.'

'Yes I do. I found about six old, mouldy lunches under her bed yesterday. If she's not careful, she'll be having visitors, and they won't be pet mice!' his mum answered.

Chapter 4

'Make sure you look after those trainers, Josh. At the price we paid, you won't be getting another pair until you're twenty-one,' Mum said as they walked back in the front door.

'Yes, Mum.'

'And clean the mouse cage and your room. Now!'

Josh scrunched his nose up and went into his bedroom. He liked it messy. Why couldn't he have his room the way he wanted? If he didn't clean it, so what?

He carried the mouse cage and a cardboard shoebox outside into the backyard. First he put the mice, Hansel and Gretel, in the shoebox and took everything out of the cage. Then he carefully put the running wheel, the plastic ball with a bell inside it and the food containers in a bucket of hot water and disinfectant.

Next, Josh took the newspaper lining out and put it in the bin. Then he wiped the bottom of the cage with a cloth he had dipped in disinfectant and put in clean newspaper. Then he put Hansel and Gretel back in the cage. He dried off the plastic toys and returned them to the cage.

Was he imagining it, or did the mice look a little bit happier? He left the mice outside for some sun and went back inside to clean his bedroom.

Josh sat on his bed. He picked up some of his clothes from the floor and put them on his bed. He found his Gameboy at the bottom of the pile. Luckily, he hadn't stepped on it. Last week he'd accused Angela of hiding it from him and they'd had a huge fight. He'd better make sure she didn't see it.

He started to play, just for a while, until he advanced another couple of levels.

Chapter 5

'Lunch-time, Josh!' His mother was calling him back to the real world.

Josh came out into the kitchen and sat at the table.

'Did you wash your hands?' she asked.

'When I was cleaning the mouse cage, I had my hands in the bucket.'

'You should have washed your hands afterwards with soap and clean water. Germs are great at survival.'

'Don't nag so much, Mum. I'm not going to die if I don't wash my hands.'

'No, but you could get a stomach bug. And the rest of us could too. I was reading in the paper today that colds are not passed through germs in the air; they're passed through touch. And not just through direct touch, but by touching something that someone with a cold has touched.'

'I haven't got a cold.'

'I know that. I'm just making a point. Wash your hands. Especially after you go to the toilet.'

'Okay, okay. Chill!'

Chapter 6

As Josh was finishing his sandwich, there was a knock at the door. It was his friend, Tim.

'Hi, Josh. I thought I'd visit you for a change. Mum said I could stay for the afternoon if you're not doing anything?'

'Just hanging around. Let's go into my room and I'll show you my footy-card collection.'

'Don't forget your gas mask, Tim!' Mum said.

'What does she mean?' Tim asked Josh.

'Nothing. My mum's one of the cleaning police. I'm thinking of trading her in for a slob.'

Standing in the doorway, Tim asked, 'Phew, what's that smell?'

'What smell?'

'The cleanliness police need a new plan. How about we look at your card collection in the family room? I'll wait there for you,' said Tim.

What was wrong with his room? Josh looked around for his card collection. There was a pile on the desk, some cards at the end of his bed, and some scattered on the floor in front of the wardrobe. For a moment, Josh stood in the doorway and tried to see the room through Tim's eyes.

At the end of his bed there was a pile of clothes, including the socks and pants he'd worn when he played footy at lunch-time yesterday. Maybe his socks smelt. He picked one up and had a whiff. A bit on the pongy side, but only if you got too close.

His Lego was spread out on the floor and a half-built space station was in the middle of the room. His carpet hadn't been vacuumed for a while, a couple of months probably. He remembered doing it at Easter because his mum had agreed to hide Easter eggs in his room if Josh cleaned it. A pancaked Easter egg was squashed into the carpet beside his desk. It was one of those eggs with caramel in the middle.

There was even a plate sticking out from under his bed. An unidentifiable leftover, covered in blue mould, oozed over it. Perhaps he should take it out to the kitchen.

A trail of breadcrumbs led nowhere in particular. Seeds, shredded paper and a couple of piles of mouse droppings dotted the floor under the stand where the mouse cage usually sat. Not so good.

After Tim went home, Josh decided to tidy up. He picked up the mouse droppings with newspaper and put them in the bin. The pancaked chocolate followed, along with the unidentifiable mould. He sorted his clothes; they were all dirty. He put them in the laundry basket and picked up his Lego, making space for it on the desk. Then Josh got the vacuum cleaner out and he actually used it. He emptied his rubbish into the wheelie bin in the backyard. His mum followed him back to his room.

'Still looking for your card collection, Josh?'

'Ha, ha, Mum. Just making space so Tim can come in.'

'Tim will have to come over more often. Once a week would probably do the trick,' chuckled Josh's mum.

'I won't need Tim to remind me, or even you, Mum. I've decided I don't want to live like a slob. I don't want people to think that I'm dirty. I feel better when I'm clean and my room is tidy.'

'It's like when you get all dressed up to go out. You feel great! I think you've learnt a lot about looking after yourself, Josh. My little boy is growing up.'

'Ohh, Mummmmm!'

Activities and Discussion

Being Responsible for Good Health

Introduce the topic by having a class discussion. Ask the students to consider:

> ▸ Why is personal hygiene important for wellbeing?
>
> ▸ What other factors help create good health? List them.
>
> ▸ What would your image of good health look like?
>
> ▸ How can you be more responsible for your own wellbeing?

Ask the students to complete the activity sheet Images of Good Health.

Growing Up

Explain to the students that our body begins to change when we approach puberty. It becomes even more important for us to be responsible and maintain good standards of personal hygiene. Ask the students to complete the activity sheet Growing Up.

Being Responsible for Wellbeing

Introduce the activity by asking the class to brainstorm and answer the questions below. (The class teacher may like to list the students' answers on the board to refer to later.)

Ask the students:

What do you think are the major influences on a young person's physical, emotional and social health?

Some suggestions are:

> ▸ the country the young person was born in
>
> ▸ their access to health services
>
> ▸ parents' income
>
> ▸ level of parental care
>
> ▸ level of parental health
>
> ▸ availability of medicines
>
> ▸ education
>
> ▸ war or violence, religion
>
> ▸ cultural beliefs
>
> ▸ friendships
>
> ▸ language barriers
>
> ▸ support networks
>
> ▸ nutrition
>
> ▸ exercise and fitness
>
> ▸ availability of clean water
>
> ▸ hygiene

- refrigeration

- sewerage systems

- being part of an extended family

- housing and shelter

- feeling a sense of belonging

- having an optimistic outlook on life and being able to make friends easily.

Ask the students to list media or sporting personalities who have impacted on their health goals or their current image of what being healthy looks like. Ask the students to explain how they have impacted upon them and if they think the image that they portray to young people is a responsible one.

Give each student a copy of the activity sheet Creating Wellbeing. Ask them to move into small groups and discuss what items they think affect their current wellbeing the most. Ask them to consider those items that they have some control over and can be responsible for.

Health Services

Introduce the activity by saying that it's useful to know about some health services in your area.

Ask the students to create a directory of ten different health services for young people, and what these services are responsible for providing.

Ask the students to list the service and a contact number on the activity sheet My Helpful Services List. The list can be copied onto card and displayed in the classroom, or the students can put it into their personal diary.

Some suggestions for the directory are:

- medical service

- dental service

- sports massage

- recreation groups

- hobby groups

- stress management or relaxation group

- counselling service

- family crisis centre

- kids help line

- hospital

- poisons information line

- ambulance

- fire brigade

- social worker.

Images of Health

Cut out a picture from a magazine, or illustrate your ideas of what a person would look like if they presented a positive image of health. Label each aspect.

Growing Up

Design a poster about the need to be responsible for our own personal hygiene and what that would look like to you, for example, showering each day.

Taking responsibility for my own hygiene would look like...

As we approach adolescence, changes occur that may have an effect on us. List some of these changes in the columns below.

Physical Changes	Emotional Changes	Social Changes

Creating Wellbeing

In a small group, select six factors that the group agrees could affect young people's wellbeing. Consider factors they could have some control over and be responsible for.

Rank the six items, from those that have the greatest impact on wellbeing to those with the least impact. (All members of the group need to agree on the order.)

1. ....

....

2. ....

....

3. ....

....

4. ....

....

5. ....

....

6. ....

....

My Helpful Services List

Service	Phone Number

Objectives

- To assist students to identify family expectations and to understand these may differ between families.

- To help students to examine roles and responsibilities and how these may affect relationships.

- To help students examine the importance of tolerance.

Factors Enhancing Resilience

- Promoting a sense of belonging and fitting in.

- Recognition of a special gift or talent.

- Promoting proactive problem-solving.

- Encouraging an optimistic sense of future.

Introduction to the Focus Value

Brainstorm with the students and create a class definition of the focus value, 'tolerance'. The students may like to use a dictionary or thesaurus to assist in defining the meaning.

With the whole class, or in small groups, discuss how the tolerance could be positively demonstrated in the classroom and the playground, and how would they know if it was not.

The Story: Sock It To Me Sam!

The story may be read to the class by the teacher, or in small groups if multiple copies have been made.

Follow the story with a class discussion. Some suggested questions are:

- What do you think being tolerant means?

- What are expectations? Give an example. How can someone's expectations of you have a positive/negative effect on your behaviour or performance?

- How did JJ demonstrate tolerance towards Sam?

- JJ had definite expectations about parents, what were some of these expectations?

- Do you think JJ's expectations of parents were reasonable?

- In what ways did Sam's expectations of parents differ from JJ's

- How did JJ's lack of tolerance of Sam's behaviour affect their friendship?

- Did Sam have expectations of JJ's behaviour as a friend? How do you think Sam was feeling when JJ said in front of the class that his party was only a joke?

- How do you think JJ was feeling when Sam introduced her to his parents as his best friend? Explain why.

Materials

- Being Tolerant activity sheet.

- Great Expectations activity sheet.

- A Speech activity sheet.

- Paper and coloured pens for designing picture storybooks.

Sock It To Me Sam!

Written by Claire Saxby
Illustrated by Lori Head

Chapter 1

Monday

My name is Jenny Johns, but everyone calls me JJ. This is my diary. We have to keep a diary for a whole week, Mr Evans, our teacher, said. A whole week. And it's going to be the longest week in history.

My best friend, Sam, won't talk to me. It's his grandma's fault. If she didn't make Sam wear socks with names on them, I'm sure he wouldn't have said it.

It might still have been okay if the socks had had his name on them, but they didn't. Sam's grandma must have bought a truckload of those socks with different names on them. Some of them have Nelson, some Finn. There's a Todd and an Isaac, a Lewis and a Ravil. None of them have Sam's name on them.

Sometimes, he even wears odd ones, and calls his feet different names. Sam says she got them 'for a song', but the only song those socks should sing is that old one that Grandad sings, 'Wish me luck as you wave me goodbye' on their way to another place.

I just wouldn't wear them, or I'd wear them inside out or something. Sam says he doesn't mind, but if he doesn't mind, why did he get so red in the face when Lee and Manny teased him? I told him to ignore them; they're just a couple of jerks. Did he listen? No way. Sometimes boys are so stupid. Instead of ignoring the comments, Sam told them he wore the socks because his family were all performers and

that's what performers wear.

Performers! Like he's done any performing. Well, apart from when we do stuff for assembly, but that's everyone together. I guess there was the time he had to present his talk for Book Week. He cartwheeled onto the teacher's desk. She sent him to the headteacher. He somersaulted off the desk and hand-flipped out the door. She gave him an F for his talk.

F for funny; F for forget it. So much for performing.

It might be different if Sam lived with his parents. I don't know where they are. When I asked him, he said they were in Leeds. Then they were in Manchester, then Sheffield.

Sam says that's what it's like when you're a performer. It's never the same place for long. Sam lives with his grandmother in Jamaica Street. She doesn't look much like a performer to me. She's little, even shorter than Sam, and she might flip a mean pancake, but that's about the limit of her performances. She spends the rest of her time reading books and writing letters to the local paper.

Some of her arguments with Mad Murphy next door are good... first class performances. But that's about the only performance you'll get in Jamaica Street. The rest of the street is mostly vacant blocks.

So why? Why did Sam open his big mouth? Why did he have to invite everyone in the class to the performance of the millennium party at his house on Friday? This Friday.

Chapter 2

Tuesday

Sam's not talking to me. All I said was that he should admit that he was making up this party thing. What if people actually believe him and turn up at his house on Friday? But he said it was all true and why didn't I believe him? I didn't want to mention all those stories he's told about his parents and all the places they go to. If that stuff was true, why wasn't he with them? Why did he have to live with his grandma? Why did his parents move so much? Every week somewhere different, sometimes everyday. What sort of job was that?

Sam was looking so cross, but a bit sad too, as though he knew what I was thinking. 'Who's organising it?' I asked. I couldn't see his grandma getting fired up about a party. She wouldn't even let us play inside without taking our shoes off. And we always had to promise to be quiet, or we'd have to play outside, even if it was raining. I shook my head. Sam said I didn't have to come if I didn't believe him.

I pretended I had something important to tell Merri and Kate, but Merri and Kate were talking about horses. They are both horse mad, but the closest they've ever been to a horse is at the local show. I bet they'd freak if they ever had to ride one.

They have collections of horse toys with coloured manes and tails. Every lunch-time, including today, they plait the tails and weave ribbons through the manes. It is as boring as, and after about five minutes I am nearly asleep.

Sam was still sitting under the tree. It must be hard not to have a family. I couldn't imagine living with my gran. My gran and grandad are okay when they visit us, but they have all these 'house rules' at their place. I'm hardly allowed to breathe without asking if it's okay! If I had to live with them, it'd probably be even worse than living with Sam's grandma.

Kate and Merri were still talking about horses, so I went back to where Sam was sitting. He wouldn't look at me. I said we could make a party and have it at my house. We could organise it together. It would be a great party and we could invite everyone. He looked up at me then, without saying a word. Then he stood up and walked away. Just like that.

What do I care? I won't be there on Friday when everyone gets to his place and realises he was making it all up.

Chapter 3

Wednesday

It was the longest day of my whole life. The whole class was buzzing.

Okay, so that's not such a loud buzz, because there are only nineteen kids in our class, but everyone was talking about Sam's party on Friday. Suddenly, everyone wanted to be his friend. And he loved it. Didn't he realise how bad things were going to be when they found out the truth?

But he played it cool. He didn't tell them anything about the party, said they just had to wait until Friday.

Everyone figured I knew all about it, because Sam was my friend. They kept asking me if I knew anything, but of course there is no party so there was nothing to tell. It didn't matter what I said. They were sure I was in on the secret and just wouldn't tell. But, even though he's not speaking to me, I couldn't bring myself to tell them that it was all made up. Sam got himself into this mess: he can get himself out of it.

At lunch-time, I sat where we usually sit together and watch everyone else. But today I was on my own. I saw Sam coming over. Here we go I thought. He's going to tell me it was all a joke and ask if I can help him fix it?

I had already started working out what I would say, but then Sam arrived. He started to say something, but before one word was out, he was surrounded. Almost the whole class was there. It was like, all of a sudden, he'd become a hero. Everyone was following him everywhere.

'Come and play with me, Sam,' 'Do you want some of my crisps, Sam?' and 'Hey Sam, come and look at this.' So that was the end of that conversation.

I had this funny feeling in my stomach, as though I had swallowed a rock or something. I wanted it to be like it was before he started talking about this stupid party.

He looks so happy when he's talking about the party, like a cat that got to the cream.

I wonder how happy he's going to be after they find out it was all a big joke. It'll be his own fault, but I sort of wish it were true, for his sake. Maybe that's why he keeps doing it. He's hoping so much that it could be true, that he's convinced himself it is.

Chapter 4

Thursday

I tried to be nice to Sam. I really did. I gave him heaps of chances to tell me that it was all a joke, but he really believes this silly party story he's made up. It was impossible. Then he told me he'd really wanted to invite the whole school. I laughed. I was still trying to work out how he thought anyone would believe that nineteen kids would fit in his house, or even his backyard, and then he started talking about the whole school! Then, as if that wasn't wild enough, he said, like he was sharing a secret with me, that his parents would be there too. It was so weird.

He was telling me about this party, which is impossible, and making stuff up as he went along. Then he'd stop halfway through sentences, saying it's all supposed to be a secret. Then he said something about how long it was since he'd seen his mum. He shut his mouth really tight and wouldn't say anymore. His face kept changing, nearly crying, then shining like tomorrow would be the best day of his life.

But how could it be? There's just no way it could be. Is there? What sort of party could he possibly have that could fit the whole school? And how could there be food for that many, even if only half of them came? Why can't he see that it just doesn't make sense to believe him? Sam stopped trying to convince me. He just said, 'Come and see for yourself.'

Well, I'm not going to. I don't want to be in that crowd when they all find out it was a joke. Some joke. I wasn't laughing. I actually felt like crying. And it wasn't like I did anything wrong. I was just trying to help Sam. He's my friend, after all. Okay, maybe I shouldn't have stood up in class and said it was a joke. But I had to try to help him, if he wouldn't help himself.

They all looked at me, then at Sam. He just looked at his book and shook his head. Now no one is talking to me. Least of all Sam.

Chapter 5

Friday

Well, school was certainly a hoot today. Everyone avoided me. They were all talking about this magic party. Sam wasn't even there. I was sure he'd realised what a mess he was in.

Mr Evans said Sam was getting ready for the party. Then Mr Evans said how much he was looking forward to going to the party too.

Mr Evans! Mr Evans is a great teacher. On any other day, I'd be really excited that he was going to be at a party, he's such a clown. But not today; I decided I'd better have once last try at convincing Sam to come clean.

As soon as school finished, I raced home and got changed. The closer I got to Sam's street, the slower I went. What would I say? How would I say it so he understood I was trying to help?

I was so distracted by my problems, I nearly got run over by a truck. The truck beeped its horn and I stopped at the last second. I sat on the curb until my heart stopped racing. Silly truck. What was it doing in the street anyway? I stood up again. What I really wanted to do was go home and just curl up in bed. But I had to help Sam.

As I turned into his street, I held my breath. I don't know why.... I guess some tiny part inside me was hoping to see or hear a party. But of course there was nothing.

Then I saw Sam sitting on his front doorstep. I wanted to run away. He's realised, I thought. Sam waved wildly when he saw me and raced over. He grabbed me by the arm.

'Promise you won't say a word!' he said. Up the path, down the hallway and around the corner he dragged me. Stopping at the back door, he tied some cloth around my eyes. It was all so fast. I opened my mouth to speak and he clapped his hand over it.

'Not one single word. Okay?' His hand stayed in place until I nodded. By now, I was sure he'd flipped. It was safer to do what he said.

Sam guided me out the back door and down the path. I could hear banging and talking, but of course I could see nothing. Then he pushed me through the back gate into the field. Pulling off the blindfold, Sam said, 'JJ, meet my parents! Mum and Dad, this is my best friend, JJ.'

In front of us were two people, smiling just like Sam does. I looked at Sam. His smile looked too big for his face. Behind his parents stood an enormous, and I mean ginormous, tent. All around it, men and women were stretching ropes and hammering. The field was full of half-built stands.

I know my mouth was open, but for probably the first time in my life I couldn't think of a single thing to say. I looked around, at Sam, at his parents, at all the people who were working.

Then I noticed something else. Every single one of them was wearing socks with different names on them. And that's when I knew that every word Sam had said was true.

This was going to be the party of the millennium!

Activities and Discussion

Being Tolerant

Introduce the activity by asking the students, in small groups, to brainstorm and answer the two questions below.

Ask the groups to list their responses and report them to the class.

The teacher may like to list the responses for later work.

1. What would be some of your expectations of a good friend? Do you need to be tolerant sometimes with friends? Explain why.

2. What would be some of your expectations of a teacher? Do you need to be tolerant of teachers sometimes? Explain why.

Ask the students to use the activity sheet Being Tolerant to list their individual expectations of a friend and a teacher.

Parental Expectations

Present the following two focus questions to small groups for discussion:

1. What are your parents/carers expectations of you in relation to your behaviour within the family and regarding household chores, roles and responsibilities?

2. Within your group, are there differing expectations for individuals in different families, or are all parental expectations basically the same? Do we need to be tolerant of different family expectations? Explain.

Ask the students to list some examples of differing parental expectations within their group. Ask each group to then rejoin the class and share their findings with the other students in the class.

At the end of the discussion, give each student a copy of the Expectations activity sheet.

Great Expectations

Introduce this activity by asking students to discuss the following four focus questions, either as a whole class or in small groups.

1. Do your expectations of people change as they grow older? Why?

2. What do you expect from your parents/carers? For example, do you expect:

   ‣ shelter and safety

   ‣ help when you need it

   ‣ a supply of food

   ‣ medical attention if needed

   ‣ transport

   ‣ money

   ‣ help with homework

   ‣ love and caring

   ‣ encouragement and guidance

   ‣ holidays

   ‣ punishment

- the washing and ironing to be done

- parents/carers to be in good mood

- a parent to show control over negative emotions

- the house to be cleaned up if a mess is made.

3. How are you tolerant of your parents/carers in the above situations if they do not meet your expectations?

4. How are your parents/carers tolerant of you if you do not meet their expectations?
   Explain your answers.

If this activity is being conducted as a class activity, then the teacher will need to list on the board as many of the student suggestions as possible.

If it is taking place in small groups, one group member will need to report the group's findings to the class once the discussion is finished. The class teacher will need to list as many suggestions as possible.

Ask the students to then individually choose the top six expectations that they have of a parent, and list them on the Great Expectations activity sheet.

Talking Tolerance

Discuss with the class that in a school setting, tolerance of other people's ideas and opinions is important – it helps us to get along together.

Ask the students to discuss in what ways tolerance is promoted and demonstrated in their class. The students can then complete the activity sheet A Speech.

Designing a Storybook

Ask the students to design a simple picture storybook that shows the value of tolerance. (Animal characters are always fun to work with.)

Ask them to show and explain their picture storybook to a younger student at their school and another family member at home.

Being Tolerant

Complete the sentences about being tolerant.

Sometimes I need to be tolerant of my friend(s) because...

Sometimes I need to be tolerant of teachers because...

Sometimes people need to be tolerant of me because...

Expectations

1. What are your parents/carers expectations of you in relation to:

    ▸   your behaviour within the family?

    ▸   household chores?

    ▸   other roles and responsibilities?

    _____

    _____

    _____

    _____

    _____

    _____

    _____

    _____

2. Are parental expectations the same for all families? Explain how they may differ.

    _____

    _____

    _____

    _____

    _____

Do you feel frustrated at times if your parents' expectations of you are different to other students' parents' expectations of them. How could you use tolerance in those times?

_____

_____

_____

_____

_____

Great Expectations

My top six expectations of a parent	My tolerance rating if they do not reach or meet my expectation (using a scale of 1-10)
1.	
2.	
3.	
4.	
5.	
6.	

What could you do to improve your tolerance rating in areas that score poorly?

A Speech

If you had to create a one-minute speech on the importance of being tolerant with other people, what points would you make?

In your short speech you might consider and include ideas about the importance of tolerance in regard to:

> ▸ academic ability

> ▸ sporting ability

> ▸ personality traits

> ▸ differing religions

> ▸ colours of skin

> ▸ countries of origin.

Summarise your ideas in point form below:

1.

2.

3.

4.

5.

6.

7.

Objectives

- ▸ To assist students to identify their individual talents.

- ▸ To help students to examine, and be aware of, the influence of others and how this influence may affect their own willingness to express their creativity. How we need to maintain our individual personalities while fitting into a group situation.

- ▸ To help students examine the importance of confidence.

Factors Enhancing Resilience

- ▸ Promoting a sense of belonging and fitting in.

- ▸ Recognition of a special gift or talent.

- ▸ Promoting proactive problem-solving.

- ▸ Encouraging an optimistic sense of future.

Introduction to the Focus Value

Brainstorm with the students and create a class definition of the focus value, 'confidence'. The students may like to use a dictionary or thesaurus to assist in defining the meaning.

With the whole class, or in small groups, discuss how confidence could be positively demonstrated in the classroom and the playground, and how they would know if it was not.

The Story: Prince Alex's Nose

The story may be read to the class by the teacher, or in small groups if multiple copies have been made.

Follow the story with a class discussion. Some suggested questions are:

- ▸ How did Alex feel at the beginning of the story, and how had his confidence level changed by the end of the story?

- ▸ Who sets the fashion trends in our society?

- ▸ How do we learn what is fashionable and what is not?

- ▸ Would you feel more confident in a group situation if you were fashionably dressed?

- ▸ Do you think being up with the fashion trends assists you to make friends? Why?

- ▸ Do other cultures consider different things to be fashionable compared with your culture? For example, it's fashionable in some cultures for women to have little feet.

- ▸ Do you think dressing in a fashionable way influences what other people think about you? Why?

- ▸ Why do you think some people feel confident when they are dressed fashionably?

Materials

- ▸ Creating a Fashion activity sheet.

- ▸ Coloured pens.

- ▸ Fashion or Comfort activity sheet.

- ▸ Being Fashionable activity sheet

- ▸ Body Language activity sheet.

Prince Alex's Nose

Written by Helen Silvester
Illustrated by Jacquie Young

Chapter 1

Prince Alex was ugly. The Prince knew he was, because his own servants told him so every day. His nose was much too small to be fashionable. His long, blonde hair was too straight and flat. He didn't even have a mole on his cheek. No matter how many frogs he kissed, he still couldn't grow a wart anywhere.

Queen Hilda, Alex's mother, was too busy to notice how he looked. His father might have helped Alex, if he hadn't died soon after Alex was born.

So Alex spent his days alone in the forest. No one knew the forest better than he. Alex always brought down the first pheasant of the season. He knew where all the best figs and wild berries grew, and he kept the palace supplied with wild flowers. But it was lonely in the forest. Alex longed for someone to share the flowers, figs and berries.

When he went into the town, he wore a hat covering his face and hair. Most people didn't look at or speak to him, but he didn't mind. He would just sit in the town market square and watch the beautiful people with their wild, upright hair and large, prominent, warty noses.

Often, he would hear them talking about Princess Fleur, from the next kingdom. Her nose was always described as the largest ever seen and her hair the wildest. Princess Fleur's looks were held to be the most striking of anyone in all the neighbouring kingdoms. This made Alex despair even more of his long, straight, golden hair and his small, pert nose.

Chapter 2

Early one morning, Alex was deep in the forest gathering the first figs of the season, when the birds became silent. Suddenly, he heard a twig snapping a short distance away. As quickly as he could, Alex grabbed hold of the branch above and pulled himself high into the tree.

Just as his foot was disappearing into the foliage, a figure dressed in hunting colours appeared. She had short, black hair that stood straight up, and three prominent moles were spread out over her large, bulbous nose. From his perch high in the fig tree, Prince Alex could see she was the most beautiful woman he had ever seen.

The woman strode to the base of the tree and looked up. 'Is that a bird I spy, or a wood spirit come to steal me away?' she called.

Alex tried to hide behind the tree trunk, not wanting to scare her away with his ugliness.

'It must be a spirit,' she said. 'I wonder if I should shoot it down?' She lifted her bow.

'Don't shoot, kind lady,' said Alex from behind the branches. 'I was just gathering figs for – er – my mother. Please continue on your way and don't let me interrupt your hunt.'

'Come down and I will help you,' said the stranger. 'For I cannot come to you. Climbing trees is one skill that I have yet to master.'

Alex stole a look, making sure his face was still in shadow. 'I don't even know who you are, lady.'

'My name is Princess Fleur and I assure you it is safe to come down, spirit.'

'I think I might stay here. It's quite comfortable,' said Prince Alex, still hiding.

Princess Fleur sat down with her back against the tree. 'Very well. How goes the fig hunt?'

Princess Fleur and Prince Alex talked until darkness fell. It was only then that Alex felt it safe to come down.

'Where do you live, spirit, that I might escort you safely to your home?' asked Princess Fleur.

'That is not necessary, kind lady. I am quite at home in the forest.' With that, Alex fled into the darkness before the moon could show his ugliness.

Chapter 3

He arrived home breathless. The castle looked just as dim and forbidding as ever, but a torch had been left burning at the drawbridge, most likely by Mr Giles, the butler.

Mr Giles was the one person who really looked after Prince Alex. Queen Hilda barely moved her eyes from the stack of papers on her desk when Alex wished her goodnight. It was Mr Giles who made sure he had dinner, and it was Mr Giles who sent him off to bed before he fell asleep over his books. However, Alex couldn't bring himself to tell Mr Giles about Princess Fleur. It was his secret.

The secret became more and more difficult to keep. Every morning, Alex disappeared into the forest. Often, he hunted pheasants or gathered berries, then, checking the Princess wasn't waiting for him, he would slip into the fig tree. The Princess would arrive about lunch-time and they would talk till dark. They discussed the forest, and their likes and dislikes.

The Princess told him all about her life and the expectations everyone placed on her. She even told him about her mother hunting for a husband for her, and how all the candidates were so conscious of their looks, continually patting their noses and warts, and dragging their fingers through their hair.

Alex was always brief answering any questions about himself. All Princess Fleur knew was that he lived in a large house with his mother, who worked long hours helping people.

One evening, as the Prince came down the tree, just before the moon rose, Princess Fleur asked, 'Would you come to my ball tomorrow evening, spirit? It would be nice to have someone there I could talk to.'

Prince Alex longed to go, but knew he couldn't risk her seeing him.

'I don't think I would fit in at a ball,' he answered. Prince Alex had never been to a ball. His mother had always been too busy to consider entertaining, and thought Alex was happy playing in the forest.

'Nonsense,' said the Princess. 'You are well-spoken and educated, and you don't fuss over your

appearance. I can tell by your voice you are the most handsome man in the kingdom.'

Princess Fleur continued to plead with Alex until the moon was appearing on the horizon. Desperate to get away, Prince Alex eventually agreed. As he ran from the clearing, the Princess called out, promising to leave an invitation at the base of the tree the next day.

Chapter 4

Alex wasn't going to go to the fig tree the next day. He moped in his room all morning until his servants noticed and asked what was wrong. Against his good judgement, he told them about Princess Fleur. Before he knew it, one servant had gone to retrieve the invitation, while the other had called for the nose peddler.

The nose peddler was a short, shabby, rat of a man. No one knew where he came from or where he went, but all knew that only the nose peddler sold the most fashionable items: dresses and garments in the latest shapes and colours, cages of frogs guaranteed to cause warts, and matching wigs for those whose hair persisted in remaining straight and shiny. Most importantly, he sold noses; noses of all shapes, but only one size: large. The little man fussed and tut-tutted around Prince Alex, commenting on his too small nose, shiny yellow hair and lack of moles or warts. Alex's servants held up samples of material, hair colouring and noses, while the nose peddler gave his opinion.

Several hours later, Prince Alex saw a fashionably dressed stranger in the mirror. He wore a large, frilled, purple outfit covered in orange stripes, finished with a matching orange wig and fan. Alex's 'new' nose was three times the size of his usual nose and topped by a large black mole with three short hairs.

He turned his head to one side to try to balance the weight of the false nose. It felt as though it was going to come off. He checked, but the nose was still there.

As Alex's servants were congratulating themselves for doing such a good job, Mr Giles came in. He stopped briefly then slowly walked around Alex. Prince Alex tried hard to stand still, even though Mr Giles's inspection made him want to throw off all the splendour.

'Are you sure?' was all Mr Giles said when he finished looking over the servants' handiwork.

When Alex nodded, Mr Giles left the room with a sigh. This made Alex want to stay at home even more, but his servants started telling him how he would be the most elegant man at the ball, and how Princess Fleur was sure to fall in love with him.

They bustled him into the waiting coach before he could change his mind. It wasn't until he was pulling up at Princess Fleur's castle that Prince Alex looked at his invitation. It was made out to The Fig Spirit and signed by Princess Fleur herself. Grasping his fan firmly, Alex promised himself that his first ball would be one to remember.

Chapter 5

A footman opened the door at the castle drawbridge. Quickly touching his nose to make sure it was still in place, Alex alighted from the carriage.

The ballroom was lit from wall to wall with candles. Mirrors were hung along the panels, making the ballroom look even larger and more crowded. Guests were lined up along the sides chatting, but Alex

could see them surreptitiously watching themselves in the mirror and patting their noses and hair.

Their reflections were forgotten when the butler announced in his booming voice, 'The Fig Spirit!'

The stares made Prince Alex feel like he wanted to run. He put his fan up to hide his blush, forgetting about the false nose.

The fan became caught in one of the huge nostrils. As Alex flicked the fan open, the false nose, with the fan still attached, flew off his face and into one of the many pot plants lining the entrance. The watching crowd gasped in horror.

Oblivious to the drama, Princess Fleur entered the ballroom from behind Alex. Tapping him on the shoulder, she exclaimed, 'My Fig Spirit, I am so glad you came. I've been hoping you would. May I have the honour of this dance?'

Not having anywhere to hide, Prince Alex bowed to Princess Fleur. Then, lifting his small, pert nose, he looked her full in the face and smiled. 'Yes please.'

Princess Fleur took Alex by the hand and led him to the centre of the room. The musicians started playing at her nod.

'I wasn't sure you would come. You've always hidden before. I'm glad you have come down from the fig tree at last.'

Prince Alex looked at Princess Fleur. She hadn't noticed his nose at all. All the other guests around the ballroom were staring at them and whispering. Princess Fleur saw Prince Alex watching the guests.

'Look at them. They are jealous of how handsome you are.'

'But my nose,' Alex stammered.

Princess Fleur looked at Alex's nose for the first time.

'Is in the middle of your face, where it should be.'

'But it's too small.'

'Your nose fits your face, as does mine,' and she squinted at the large hairy moles on the end of her bulbous nose. Princess Fleur looked again at Prince Alex's nose. 'You know, you remind me of some of the portraits of my ancestors. They had regal little noses like yours. I wouldn't be surprised if your nose became fashionable again soon.'

Prince Alex looked at the people lining the walls as he and Princess Fleur danced past. Here and there, the guests were taking off their noses and rubbing their faces with relief. The pot plants were littered with false noses. Talking excitedly about the newest thing in noses, people surrounded Princess Fleur and Prince Alex. Grabbing Alex's hand, Princess Fleur walked him out into the garden.

'Enough about noses. How many figs did you gather today, spirit? Or are you going to tell me your real name now?'

Laughing, Prince Alex told Princess Fleur his real name, and how many figs he had gathered that day. None.

The two of them talked about many things that night, but noses were never ever mentioned again.

The next day, a small rat of a man was seen leaving the kingdom with a collection of large noses and several red marker pens in his possession. In his pocket was a letter attached to a newspaper clipping celebrating the birth of a princess two kingdoms away, where the fashion was bushy eyebrows and small pointed noses.

The clipping described the infant as having a large, oversized nose and two red moles. The man whistled as he walked. The baby's parents had employed him to set the fashion in their kingdom for the next eighteen years.

Activities and Discussion

Creating a Fashion

Ask the students to create a new fashion for students to wear at school. Ask them to draw their design on the activity sheet Creating a Fashion and to write a marketing caption for their new design as well.

Fashion Through the Ages

Ask the students to list and draw five items that have been fashionable over the past century.
For example:

- ▶ feather boas for ladies
- ▶ beehive hair styles
- ▶ corsets
- ▶ bathing caps
- ▶ pointed shoes
- ▶ slicked down hair
- ▶ smoking jackets for men
- ▶ platform shoes

Ask the students to share their list with a friend.

Compile a class list and then, as a whole class, discuss the reasons for the different fashions and whether we think that people were always comfortable.

Ask the students to complete the activity sheet Fashion or Comfort.

Who Am I?

Discuss and list with the class what is currently fashionable in clothes and music.

Split the students into groups and distribute the activity sheet Being Fashionable. Discuss the group responses.

Confident Body Language

Introduce this activity by saying that body language is very important when communicating a feeling of confidence to others.

On the activity sheet Body Language ask students to draw a confident looking student. Ask them to identify and label the body language that shows confidence, for example, standing tall and making eye contact.

Creating a Fashion

My new fashion design

My marketing caption is:

Fashion or Comfort

Think about fashion versus comfort. List some reasons for and against.

For	Against

Would you rather be fashionably dressed or comfortably dressed? Why?

_____

_____

_____

How do you think dressing a particular way may affect your confidence?

_____

_____

_____

In your opinion, how does a confident person look?

_____

_____

_____

Does feeling confident have anything to do with being fashionable? Explain.

_____

_____

_____

_____

_____

Being Fashionable

List the current fashionable clothing labels and music groups. Then list some items that are fashionable in your peer group

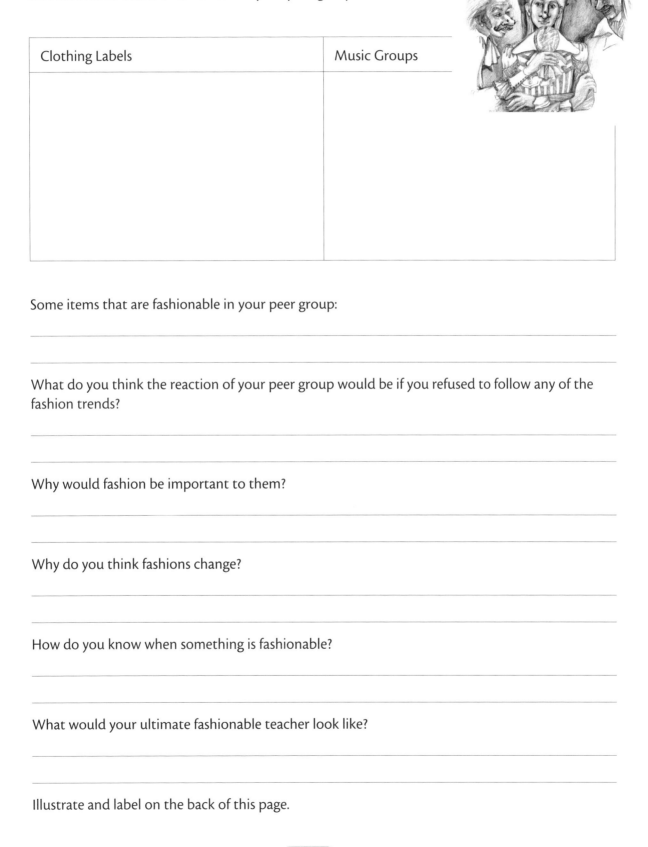

Clothing Labels	Music Groups

Some items that are fashionable in your peer group:

_____

_____

What do you think the reaction of your peer group would be if you refused to follow any of the fashion trends?

_____

_____

Why would fashion be important to them?

_____

_____

Why do you think fashions change?

_____

_____

How do you know when something is fashionable?

_____

_____

What would your ultimate fashionable teacher look like?

_____

_____

Illustrate and label on the back of this page.

Body Language

Draw and label a confident looking student.

Objectives

- To help students examine the influence of the media and peer pressure on health goals and behaviours.

- To help students develop strategies for making healthy food choices, taking into account factors such as nutrition, growth, energy and positive body image.

- To help students examine the importance of respect.

Factors Enhancing Resilience

- Promoting a sense of belonging or fitting in.

- Promoting proactive problem-solving.

- Enhancing a positive social orientation.

Introduction to the Focus Value

Brainstorm with the students and create a class definition of the focus value, 'respect'. The students may like to use a dictionary or thesaurus to assist in defining the meaning.

With the whole class, or in small groups, discuss how respect could be positively demonstrated in the classroom and the playground, and how they would know if it was not.

The Story: All Shapes and Sizes

The story may be read to the students by the class teacher, or in small groups if multiple copies have been made.

Follow the story with a class discussion. Some suggested questions are:

Describe what the term 'body image' means to you.

- How important do you think having a positive body image is to participating in and enjoying life? Explain.

- What are some of the elements of a positive body image?

- Describe what a positive body image and a negative body image would look like for you?

- How can body image be affected by diet and exercise? Any other factors?

- Is there a specific age when body image becomes more important to people? Explain.

- What negative effects could poor body image have upon a person?

- How do you show respect towards your body?

Materials

- Body Image activity sheet.

- Pictures Describing Me activity sheet.

- Magazines, newspapers and glue.

- Influences activity sheet.

- Respecting The Body activity sheet.

All Shapes and Sizes!

Written by Leanne Winfield
Illustrated by Katie Jardine

Chapter 1

On Saturday morning, Priti and her younger brother, Ravi, and older sister, Rachita, were watching CD: UK while eating breakfast. The Sugar Babes were performing their new song Push The Button.

'Don't they sound great?' said Priti.

'I think they look fantastic! I want one of their outfits,' declared Rachita.

'They're too skinny,' Ravi said. 'They look like stick insects. Just like you, Rachita!'

'They're not too thin! They look fantastic. I want to look just like them!' Rachita yelled.

'You already do!' Ravi yelled back at her.

'Stop it, Ravi,' Priti said. 'Rachita can look any way she wants.'

'Butt out, chubby,' Ravi retorted as he stormed back into the kitchen with his plate.

'There's a photo of The Sugar Babes in Heat Magazine,' Rachita said, turning the pages of the magazine. 'Don't worry about Ravi. He's just grumpy because he got flattened at footy training last night. He needs to build up some muscles.'

'He's only ten! Give him some time! Oh, aren't these dresses great? But look at the size of the models. They're so tiny. I bet I'd never fit into those dresses.'

Priti looked at the roundness of her own body. It made her feel awkward. The pictures of models in the magazine, and the singers and dancers on television, made her feel even more like a chubby bear.

'Don't be so negative. Let's ask Mum to take us shopping and we'll try on some dresses.'

Chapter 2

Mum left Priti and Rachita to browse in Top Shop while she went to the bank and did some shopping.

'What colour would you like? I think the bluey-green one would suit you,' Rachita advised, handing Priti a dress.

'What size is it?' Priti asked. 'I hate getting into the change room and finding out I've got the wrong one when I'm half undressed.'

'It'll fit,' Rachita said. 'Come on, let's go.'

Priti trailed along behind Rachita to the changing rooms. Rachita danced into the first cubicle and Priti scowled as she went into the second.

'Come out when you've got the dress on,' Rachita said.

Priti took her top and trousers off, avoiding looking in the mirror. She pulled the dress over her head. It was a bit of a stretch to get it on. She wriggled, tugged and squirmed. Then she looked in the mirror. The dress was a bit lumpy over her hips and the zip wouldn't quite do up. It was baggy in the shoulders and she couldn't move her arms. Why didn't they make clothes that fitted? Why was her body so lumpy?

'I really like this dress. I think pink is my colour, don't you, Priti? Priti? What are you doing?' Rachita called. 'Come out and show me your dress.'

'No, I don't want to. It looks hideous! I hate it.'

'If you don't come out, I'm going to crawl underneath the door,' Rachita threatened.

'All right. A quick look and then I'm taking it off and going home. I'm never going shopping again!'

Priti opened the door and stepped out. Several other shoppers who had overheard their conversation turned around to look. Priti tried to smooth down the dress, but it bunched up around her curves.

'Oh! I look like a pink plank of wood with arms,' moaned Priti.

'It must be a bad cut. What about some jeans? Everyone can wear jeans.'

'No, I hate jeans. They're not comfortable. They don't fit me. I don't want to shop anymore. I'll meet you out the front.' Priti stormed out.

Chapter 3

At home, Priti stomped off to hide in her bedroom. On the way, she stopped in the bathroom to wash her hands. How much did she weigh? She stood on the scales. Too much! No change from yesterday, but a bit more than last week.

Rachita came in to wash her hands too. Priti jumped off the scales before Rachita could look at her weight.

'I wonder how much I weigh,' Rachita said as she took Priti's place. 'Too much!' Sighing, she walked away.

'What are you doing?' Mum asked as she came into the bathroom. 'How much do I weigh?' she asked, stepping onto the scales. 'Too much!'

'We were just checking our weight,' Rachita said.

'Whatever for?' Mum asked.

'For the same reason that you do every morning,' Rachita replied.

'Oh, right.' After a pause, she added, 'Perhaps it's not such a good habit to get into.' Then, with a thoughtful expression, Mum headed for the kitchen.

Priti went into her bedroom, put her iPod on, pulled out a packet of crisps, and flopped on the bed to listen to some music. When the song she was listening to had finished and the crisp packet was empty, she turned the iPod off. A few minutes later, a car pulled into the driveway. Wondering who might be visiting at lunchtime, she ventured out into the kitchen. Mum was putting on the kettle and Aunty Susan was settling herself down at the table.

'And how are you, Priti?' Aunty Susan asked.

'Okay,' Priti said.

'She's had a bad morning at the clothes shop. Nothing will fit,' volunteered Mum.

'We all have those days,' Aunty Susan said. 'People come in all shapes and sizes. I see them in my work as a dietician. I always say that the important thing is to be healthy.'

'What is healthy?' Priti asked.

'Not being too overweight. Eating fresh fruit and vegetables, some meat and fish and dairy. It's about balance and control. Sometimes, it can be easy to eat the whole pack of sweets, or more than one slice of cake, but do you really need it?'

'I need to hear this too,' Mum said rubbing her own round belly.

'But look at Rachita and me. We are almost opposites. And Ravi's sort of in between. Does that make Ravi the normal, healthy one?'

'Not necessarily,' Aunty Susan replied. 'He's probably more active than you and Rachita.'

'But I do more exercise than Rachita,' Priti protested. ' I play netball every week. Rachita doesn't play any sport, and she's so skinny.'

'You probably have a healthier appetite than Rachita. And the fact that you exercise regularly has to make you healthier. Lots of factors come into body shape: how tall you are, your metabolism, your age and hormones.'

'What are hormones?' queried Rachita, coming into the kitchen.

'Things that regulate how your body works. Exercise and diet do have an effect on your body size, but the important thing is to understand that we're all different in shape and size, and to be happy with your own body.'

Still puzzled, Priti asked, 'What's metabolism?'

'How your body processes food. Some people have a fast metabolism and some have a slow metabolism.'

'I bet mine's slow,' Priti said.

'Mine must be slow too,' commented Rachita.

'You're probably just at an awkward age, Priti. And perhaps you're between sizes. You'll feel better when you grow a bit more,' Aunty Susan said reassuringly.

'Thanks, but that doesn't help me now,' Priti said, taking out a tub of yoghurt and a packet of crisps. 'Come on, Priti. Let's eat outside,' suggested Rachita, picking up an apple.

'Rachita!' Mum called. 'You need more than an apple for lunch. And Priti, leave the crisps behind. Come and get a sandwich, both of you!'

'It's okay, Mum. One packet of crisps won't hurt me. And Rachita can't hear you,' said Priti as she closed the door.

Chapter 4

At dinnertime, Priti helped Mum cut up the vegetables for a stir-fry. Dad arrived home from his golf game and gave Mum a kiss and a cuddle, then messed up Priti's hair as he walked past her.

'How's my girl?' he asked. 'What did you do today?'

'Not much, I've been bored,' Priti said.

'You need to do something active. How about we have a game of golf tomorrow?'

'Great idea,' Mum said. 'We can have a picnic lunch afterwards!'

'A picnic lunch sounds like fun. But golf? I don't know, Dad,' Priti replied.

'Come on! We'll all go to the golf course and have a hit! Get us all out in the fresh air and sunshine.'

'Okay. But I can't see you talking Rachita into it.'

'We'll do our best,' Dad said.

After dinner, the girls sat in the lounge watching telly while Dad and Ravi did the dishes.

'Is Rachita coming to play golf tomorrow?' Ravi asked Dad.

'She said she would think about it,' Dad replied.

'Sometimes Rachita worries me, Dad. She doesn't eat enough food. She hardly touched her stir-fry,' Ravi said as he scraped the remains off Rachita's plate into the bin.

'Priti's like Mum, isn't she? Neither of them has left any scraps. Mum's pretty big. Does that bother you, Dad?'

'I think your mother looks beautiful no matter what size she is. But it's up to her to feel good about herself. Some people are thin and don't feel good about themselves.'

'Like Rachita?' Ravi interrupted.

'I think Rachita feels okay about herself. She's just going through a stage where she's not eating properly. We might have to help her a bit.'

'How?' Ravi asked.

'I'm not sure. Perhaps we could ask her to make us a healthy, afternoon treat if she doesn't come to golf with us.'

Chapter 5

Three weeks later, Priti's family was preparing to leave for the family golf day.

Mum was making sandwiches, Priti was packing the fruit, Dad was organising the drinks and Rachita was putting the treat she had made the night before in a tin. Ravi was in the laundry getting the icebox.

Priti went into the bathroom to wash her hands. She looked around for the scales.

'What are you doing?' Rachita asked.

'Looking for the scales. Oh, I forgot that Mum has thrown them out.'

'Um, it's a good thing. We don't need to know how much we weigh. You look great anyway, Priti!'

'Thanks. I feel so much better since I started training with the swimming team and playing golf with Dad on Saturdays. No more sneaking packets of crisps into my room! And you look great too, Rachita. Perhaps I'll sign up for the next swimming competition alongside you.'

'Don't get too good, will you? Anyway, I do feel better. I've got more energy and I know I'm eating healthy food.'

'Did you girls wash your bathers and towels out after training?' Mum asked. 'I'm just doing mine, Ravi's and your father's.

'Yes, we did our bathers earlier. The towels are in the laundry basket,' replied Priti.

'We want them clean and ready to use for Tuesday morning swimming training for The Lucerone Family Swim Team. All fit and healthy!' Mum declared.

'And still all different shapes and sizes!' Priti said happily.

Activities and Discussion

Body Image

Have a class discussion and introduce the topic to the students by suggesting that our concept of body image may be influenced by the media or by peer pressure.

Suggest that sometimes what we see as a 'cool' body image may not be very good for our health.

The class discussion can include questions such as:

- How do you think magazines, TV and movies influence the way we feel about, and treat, our bodies?

- Do you compare yourself to people on TV and in magazines? Why or why not?

- Do you get stressed about your clothes when you are going to attend a special event?

- Do you feel that how you look influences how people treat you?

- How do you treat your body respectfully? List some of the things you do that show you respect your body.

- Where do you think the pressure to look good comes from?

- What do you think is more important: the way you look or what sort of person you are?

Distribute the activity sheet Body Image. After completion discuss what points have been identified.

Pictures Describing Me

Using magazines and newspapers, ask the students to cut out pictures of activities that they enjoy doing, and words that describe the type of person they are, for example, creative or sporty. Ask them to paste them onto the activity sheet Pictures Describing Me to create a mosaic effect.

Ask the students to write on the back of the activity sheet, about how the selected pictures demonstrate the different ways they respect themselves.

Influences

Ask the students to list some of the factors that may influence the way they feel about their body, for example, magazines, newspapers, TV, movies, friends and parents.

Ask them to rate each component out of ten points, starting with the factor that affects them the most, on the Influences activity sheet.

Healthy Eating and Exercise

Introduce this topic by discussing what constitutes a healthy diet. Both a healthy die and exercise can help us feel good about ourselves.

Ask he students to complete the activity sheet Respecting The Body.

Body Image

Draw a person displaying a positive body image. Identify and label the parts of your drawing that demonstrate a positive body image.

Pictures Describing Me

Paste your cuttings to create a mosaic effect. On the back of the sheet, write about how your selected pictures demonstrate the different ways you respect yourself.

Influences

Rate each factor out of 10.

0 = no influence and 10 = a tremendous amount of influence.

Factor	Rating

Explain the reasons behind your scores to a partner or small group of students.

Respecting The Body

Create a week-long healthy exercise plan for a student your age.

Make it varied to keep it interesting. Have a backup plan for changing weather conditions.

Exercise Plan		
Day	**Exercise**	**Backup Plan**
Monday		
Tuesday		
Wednesday		
Thursday		
Friday		
Saturday		
Sunday		

The way we care for our bodies demonstrates the level of respect we have for ourselves.

Objectives

▸ To help students understand that anxiety and worry can affect us all at various times in our lives.

▸ To help students become aware of strategies that may help to calm us in anxiety producing situations.

▸ To help students examine the importance of courage.

Factors Enhancing Resilience

▸ Promoting proactive problem-solving.

▸ Encouraging an optimistic sense of future.

▸ Promoting a sense of belonging and fitting in.

Introduction to the Focus Value

Brainstorm with the students and create a class definition of the focus value, 'courage'. The students may like to use a dictionary or thesaurus to assist in defining the meaning.

With the whole class, or in small groups, discuss how courage could be positively demonstrated in the classroom and the playground, and how they would know if it was not.

The Story: Samuel The Brave

The story may be read to the students by the teacher, or in small groups if multiple copies have been made.

Follow the story with a class discussion. Some suggested questions are:

▸ What caused Samuel to feel very anxious in the story?

▸ How did Samuel's behaviour show that he was very anxious?

▸ Where in the story did Samuel show courage? Explain.

▸ What type of thing makes you feel anxious or worried? Give examples.

▸ How do you use courage to overcome your fears?

▸ What strategies do you use to calm yourself down when you are feeling anxious, worried or frightened about something?

Materials

▸ My Body's Anxiety Indicators activity sheet.

▸ Calm Down Ideas activity sheet.

▸ Courage Comic activity sheet.

▸ My Courageous Story activity sheet.

Samuel the Brave

Written by Helen Miles
Illustrated by Ian Moule

Chapter 1

Samuel heard thunder rumble in the distance. 'I have to go home,' he said to his friend. 'There's a storm coming!'

'Are you scared again?' Johan asked. 'You're frightened of everything!'

Samuel ran home, rushed up to his room, slammed the door and grabbed his teddy bear.

Boooom! Ruuumble! Craaash!

Lightning lit up his room. Samuel covered his eyes. Thunder crashed again. He pulled his quilt over his head. Rain pelted on the roof and blew in through his open window. He hid under the bed. The house creaked and groaned. He scrambled into his wardrobe. He heard loud noises downstairs, so he crawled behind his clothes.

Bang! The wind slammed his wardrobe door open. Samuel gasped. But then he heard a different noise … a muffled scream from somewhere outside. He pulled the clothes away from his head and listened. In the distance, he could hear a faint voice, a lady's voice, yelling for help.

What if Mum was in trouble? Maybe she'd been hit by lightning. Or maybe she had slipped on the wet path.

Samuel poked his head out of the wardrobe. The lightning cracked, and he hesitated. Then, taking a deep breath, he ran to his window and banged it shut. He peered out through the rain.

The sky grumbled and Samuel shook. It was all too scary. But just before he turned to scurry back to his wardrobe, something caught his eye… something red in the next-door neighbour's garden. He squinted, trying to make out what it was. An arm waved in the air. It was Mrs McCall, on the ground, crying for help!

Chapter 2

Someone will hear her soon, Samuel thought, blinking at the old lady. Another thunderclap boomed overhead. He sat cuddling his teddy bear as the minutes passed. Samuel took another peek outside. Mrs McCall still lay on the ground. Perhaps she's passed out, or maybe she's dead, Samuel thought, wringing his hands.

Opening his bedroom door, he screamed for his mother. No answer. He screamed for his father. No answer. Where were they? What do I do now? he

worried. He couldn't possibly leave poor old Mrs McCall out in the storm any longer … could he?

I know! I'll ring an ambulance, he thought with relief. I don't have to go outside at all! But when Samuel picked up the phone, the line was dead.

His teddy bear stared at him. Samuel could almost hear him saying, 'Don't be afraid, I'll come with you. Go and help your neighbour.'

It will only take a minute, Samuel thought, and ran downstairs, Teddy clutched under his arm.

The wind and rain attacked them when Samuel opened the back door. He staggered outside, his heart thumping. Soaking wet and frightened, he tucked Teddy into his jacket, climbed the fence and ran to his neighbour's side.

'Mrs McCall!' he said, tapping her shoulder. 'Are you all right?'

She groaned and lifted her head. 'Oh, Samuel. You shouldn't be out in the storm … but I'm glad you're here,' she said weakly. 'My little dog Charlie… storm frightened him … escaped … I tripped…'

Samuel scanned the garden and the swinging, side gate.

'Must find him,' Mrs McCall said. 'Help me up please.'

Both shaking, Samuel assisted Mrs McCall to stand.

Her right leg gave way and she stumbled. 'Think I've hurt my hip, and I'm very dizzy,' she said.

'I'll help you inside,' Samuel said. 'And I can ring your doctor.

'No, no! We must find Charlie first. He will be terrified. Although, the storm doesn't seem as bad now,' Mrs McCall said.

Samuel didn't want to find Charlie. What if Charlie bit him? Besides, he wanted to go inside, out of the storm. But Mrs McCall was right, the thunder and lightning seemed to be moving away.

'I suppose I could look in the front garden,' Samuel said.

After staggering inside and helping Mrs McCall to a chair, Samuel ran to the front garden. He peeked under bushes, looked under the porch and even searched in the fountain.

'I can't find him,' Samuel reported, shaking.

'Oh dear,' Mrs McCall said. A tear plopped onto her cardigan.

Samuel frowned. He pulled Teddy out from his jacket. 'Here, you can hold Teddy while I look a bit more.'

Chapter 3

Samuel walked down the street yelling, 'Charlie …Chaaaarrlliie…'

Just as the sun peeped through the clouds, a little old man lurched across the street. He's coming straight for me, Samuel thought. And he looks mean!

'Are you looking for Mrs McCall's little Charlie?' asked the old man. 'I couldn't catch him. I'm too slow these days. But he went down that way,' the old man said, pointing to the end of the street. Samuel nodded and ran off.

Now that the thunder and lightning had stopped, Samuel felt much braver. But when he turned the corner, another loud noise made him shudder. A giant machine was digging up the road! Samuel cringed against a fence and covered his ears.

'I can't go any further. It's too scary.' But then something caught his eye, a little white tail sticking out from under the machine.

'Oh no! It's Charlie!' Samuel gasped. 'The huge wheels are going to run him over!'

He screamed at the driver. 'Stop! There's a little… '

But the machine inched further forward.

Samuel took off his jacket and waved it in the air. 'Hey! Over here!'

The driver smiled and waved.

'No! No! Stop!' Samuel yelled. He pointed under the machine and shook his head.

The engine ground to a halt and the driver jumped down. 'What's wrong, young fella?' he asked.

'Charlie is under your machine,' replied Samuel.

The driver's faced turned white. 'Oh, it's just a dog,' he sighed with relief as Samuel pulled Charlie out.

'The storm frightened him and he escaped,' Samuel explained.

The driver scratched his head. 'He must have been hiding under there when I arrived.'

Charlie whimpered and hid his head under Samuel's arm. 'It's all right boy.'

Samuel thanked the driver and headed back to Mrs McCall's house.

'Hey, Samuel!' Johan shouted. 'How come you're wet and what are you doing, with Charlie? You don't like dogs.'

Samuel explained what had happened.

'I'm impressed!' said Johan, slapping Samuel on the back.

Chapter 4

Mrs McCall's worried face turned to the boys as they opened the back door.

'Thank you so much, Samuel,' she cried cuddling her dog. 'You're a little devil Charlie!'

After a tap on the door, Samuel's mother poked her head into the room.

'There you are!' she said to her son. 'We arrived back and couldn't find you.'

Samuel scowled. 'Well, I couldn't find you either. Where were you?'

'We saw Charlie escape and went to find him,' Samuel's father said. 'But I see he came back.'

Johan put his arm around Samuel's shoulder. 'Nope. Charlie didn't come back. Samuel saved him from a big roadwork machine.'

'Really? You went near a noisy machine?' asked Samuel's father.

'And your brave boy came out in the storm and helped me inside after I slipped and hurt my hip,' Mrs McCall added.

'Out in the storm!' exclaimed Samuel's mother. 'But you're frightened of animals, loud machines and, especially, storms.'

Mrs McCall turned to Samuel. 'Well, storms can be dangerous. I don't like them either, Samuel. Thank you for leaving Teddy with me, he was a great comfort.'

While Samuel's mother rang the doctor, Johan and Samuel walked outside into the sunshine.

'Come on, Samuel The Brave. Let's go and play!' said Johan.

Anxiety Indicators

Ask the students to draw a picture of themselves on the activity sheet My Body's Anxiety Indicators. Ask them to label five parts of the body, using arrows, that give you clues as to when you are feeling anxious or frightened, for example, butterflies in your stomach.

Feeling Calm

Explain to the students that it is easier to use courage to try something new when you feel calm.

On the activity sheet Calm Down Ideas, ask the students to list as many strategies as they can for calming yourself down when you feel anxious or upset. For example, taking a few deep breaths, going for a walk or listening to some music.

Courage Comic

Discuss with the class:

How has using courage helped you in a situation?

Using the activity sheet Courage Comic, ask the students to design a cartoon strip where the main character demonstrates courage. Discuss the cartoons, identifying different ways of being courageous.

Brag Wall

Explain to the class that they are going to create a courage 'brag wall' in their classroom.

Ask the students to write their courageous story on the activity sheet My Courageous Story. Ask them to cut it out and paste it onto a coloured or decorated background. These are then placed onto the class brag wall.

My Body's Anxiety Indicators

Draw a picture of yourself and, using arrows, label five parts of the body that give you clues as to when you are feeling anxious or frightened.

Write about a time you used courage to overcome anxiety and achieve something that was important to you.

_____

_____

_____

_____

_____

_____

Calm Down Ideas

List some strategies for calming yourself down when you feel anxious or upset.

1. _____

_____

2. _____

_____

3. _____

_____

4. _____

_____

5. _____

_____

What do you do at home that helps you to relax? List three things.

1. _____

_____

2. _____

_____

3. _____

_____

Discuss your list with a partner or a group.

Why is it easier to attempt something when you are calm, rather than anxious?

_____

_____

_____

_____

_____

_____

Courage Comic

Design a cartoon comic strip for a younger child, where the main character uses courage to overcome a problem.

My Courageous Story

Write your courageous story and then cut it out.

Objectives

▸ To help students identify major values they consider when deciding right from wrong behaviour.

▸ To help students identify major influences on behaviour.

▸ To help students examine the importance of determination.

Factors Enhancing Resilience

▸ Promoting a sense of belonging and fitting in.

▸ Promoting proactive problem-solving.

▸ Enhancing a positive social orientation.

Introduction to the Focus Value

Brainstorm with the students and create a class definition of the focus value, 'determination'. The students may like to use a dictionary or thesaurus to assist in defining the meaning.

With the whole class, or in small groups, discuss how determination could be positively demonstrated in the classroom and the playground, and how they would know if it was not.

The Story: Streaky Road Dash

The story may be read by the class teacher, or in small groups if multiple copies have been made.

Follow the story with a class discussion. Some suggested questions are:

▸ Does competition bring out the best in people? Explain.

▸ How important is winning to you? Discuss.

▸ What would you have done if you were in Samantha's situation in the race when Rodney fell?

▸ Can parental expectations have a positive effect on you? Can they have a negative effect? Explain.

▸ Can you think of other people in the community that also have expectations of you? For example, teachers, grandparents, coaches. Are they realistic expectations? Why? Why not?

▸ Good sportsmanship is a thing of the past.' Discuss this statement.

▸ What part does determination play in achieving personal goals? Explain.

Materials

▸ Decisions activity sheet.

▸ Goals activity sheet.

▸ Personal Values activity sheet.

Streaky Road Dash

Written by Helen Miles
Illustrated by Ian Moule

Chapter 1

Samantha's hands shook as she attempted to tie her trainer laces for the third time. Unaware of the late morning sunshine or the happy voices filtering through her window, she frowned.

She couldn't think of anything but the race, and how much she wanted to win this year. It had nothing to do with the prize of two cinema passes. She wanted to beat Rodney Andrews, her next-door neighbour.

After running second to him for the last two years, she was sick, sick, sick of him reminding her at every opportunity what a great runner he was. Living right next door made it almost impossible to ignore his mean remarks.

Only yesterday, he and his friends had swaggered up to her as she finished her training run.

'Got new trainers, slowcoach?' Rodney asked, sniggering. 'They won't do you any good. I'll still win, as usual.'

'We'll see,' Samantha said, crouched over, panting, with her hands on her knees. She straightened up, turned her back on Rodney's smirking face, and headed for her front door.

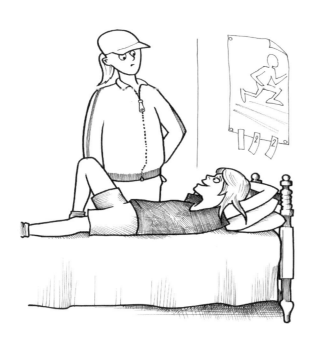

Chapter 2

After having trained hard nearly every day after school for the previous two months, Samantha had felt she had a good chance of winning … that was until today, when all self-belief seemed to evaporate.

'You'll beat Rod. I just know it!' her friend Maria said. 'He hasn't trained as hard as you.' She flopped onto Samantha's bed. 'And none of the other kids in Streaky Road are any competition, especially me.'

Samantha smiled at her friend and wished she felt as confident. She wiped her clammy hands on her tracksuit and, taking deep breaths, tried to control her quickening heartbeat.

'We're leaving now!' Samantha yelled towards the kitchen.

'Okay!' her mother called back. 'We'll see you at the starting line.'

Chapter 3

Neighbours and friends already lined the road, just as on previous years, and for a moment Samantha's thoughts turned to when she and Maria had first entered the race. They had only been five years old, and Maria had come in last, just as she'd come last every race in the six years since. But being her cheery self, she hadn't minded at all. She'd seemed happy just to participate and enjoy the barbeque afterwards. And so had Samantha, that is, until Rodney had started crowing like a rooster about his 'champion' status.

Samantha's legs felt like jelly. She swilled water around her dry mouth and started her warm-up exercises.

'Go get 'em ladies!' Mr Cheng shouted, sitting on his fold-up chair, with both thumbs up in the air.

'Thanks!' Maria said to her neighbour and turned to Samantha. 'Look how many people are here! Some of the mums have even set up stalls with food and drink.'

'Hmm,' mumbled Samantha, barely noticing the crowd or the little makeshift stalls.

'We even have a banner this year!' exclaimed Maria, pointing to the starting line.

Streaky Road Dash – Have Fun Kids!

Fun! thought Samantha. I'm not sure if this is fun any more. I'm soooo-ooo nervous.

She saw Rodney pumping his legs up and down in the air and making a big production of his arrival. As usual, his father barked instructions from the sidelines.

Just as the competitors were announced for her race, Samantha's mother, father and younger brother James rushed to her side.

'Just do your best, Sammie,' her mother encouraged, taking Samantha's tracksuit top.

'Beat him good!' said James. He threw a dirty look in Rodney's direction.

Samantha's father laughed. 'That's enough, James,' he said, but whispered in his daughter's ear, 'Although it would be good to wipe that smirk off Rodney's father's face once and for all.'

'Dad!' Samantha exclaimed.

Her mother raised her eyebrows and hauled her husband and son away.

'All competitors to the starting line!' a voice boomed out. Perspiration dripped down Samantha's back. She pulled her baseball cap further over her eyes and tried to focus on staying calm.

Maria gave Samantha's arm a gentle squeeze. 'Good luck,' she whispered.

'You too,' Samantha replied.

Chapter 4

The starter's red flag fluttered high in the air. Samantha gulped a few deep breaths.

'On your marks…' The competitors crouched down in their starting positions. Samantha's heart thumped wildly.

'Get set!' You could have heard a pin drop, and Samantha's stiff arms trembled on the road surface. She tried to concentrate on her breathing.

'GOOooo! A red flash streaked downwards, and they were off!

Samantha started well, her wobbly legs suddenly strong and her nervousness vanishing. As she pounded the familiar surface, she saw Rodney out in front, arms a blur at his sides. Everyone else was behind her… she was second. But not for long, she thought, as she closed the gap.

Gaining on him, she heard Rodney puffing and panting. His head turned slightly and she knew he'd seen her out of the corner of his eye. He increased his speed. She did the same.

They were level now, both drenched in perspiration and grunting with exertion.

Samantha willed her legs to go faster.

They ran, stride for stride, and were nearly at the

finish line … and that's when it happened. Rodney veered over towards her. His foot rammed into hers. She stumbled, but regained her balance. And suddenly he disappeared.

She was on her own! She was going to win! But the scream finally registered, and she hesitated. Taking a quick glance behind, she saw Rodney sprawled on the ground, holding his ankle.

Thoughts tumbled through her brain in a split second. He tried to trip me, serves him right! I should go back, he's hurt. But I want to win… but… but…

In those few moments of hesitation, another figure passed Samantha. She saw Rodney's father rush to his side, and as she started running again she heard him yelling at his son.

'What happened? You loser! You let a girl beat you!'

Samantha put everything she had into the last few feet and bolted over the finish line.

'Second place!' someone yelled.

Samantha looked around, wondering who had passed her. She couldn't believe she had come second again. And it was all Rodney's fault. If only he hadn't tried to trip her, and if only she hadn't hesitated, she knew she would have beaten him fair and square. But that was just like Rodney. If he couldn't get his own way honestly, he would resort to just about anything in order to win.

And she had been silly enough to worry about him being hurt!

Samantha wiped her brow and moved over to the noisy crowd that huddled around the winner. Everyone spoke at once as she edged her way through.

'Well done!'

'Congratulations!'

'Way to go!'

Samantha had her hand out ready to congratulate the winner when she was almost bowled off her feet by a huge bear hug.

'I won!' cried Maria. 'Can you believe it?'

'No! I mean yes! Oh, whatever!' said Samantha, and the two friends jumped around together in a very sweaty victory dance.

Chapter 5

'This is nearly as good as winning myself,' thought Samantha. She and Maria, along with the girl who came in third place, posed for the local newspaper photographer.

'Girlpower!' Maria yelled, holding Samantha's hand up in the air as the camera clicked.

At the barbeque later, and amongst loud cheering, especially from Samantha, Maria was presented with her prize.

'These are for you and me,' she said, handing one of the cinema passes to Samantha. 'We both won today. Now let's eat. I'm starving!'

'Rodney's mother just told me that he's injured his ankle quite badly,' Samantha's mother said as she passed a bowl of potato salad to Maria.

'Poor kid,' Samantha's father said. 'His father has probably got him up on his one good leg training him for next year's race already.'

'Well, I don't feel sorry for him at all,' Maria said, scowling. 'He didn't deserve to win. Everyone knows that I only won

because of what he did to you, Sammie,' she said, chewing on a chop. 'I saw everything. He tried to trip you. And I decided then that if you couldn't win, I was going to do it for you.' She wiped tomato sauce off her chin and looked down. 'I'm glad my stumpy little legs grew longer this year. It was so good not coming last again!'

'Yes, it's wonderful Maria,' Samantha's mother said and smiled. 'And I'm so pleased for you. But it wouldn't hurt to go and see how Rodney is.'

'No way!' yelled Maria. 'But then, I suppose we could go and rub it in a bit.'

'I have a feeling he already regrets what he did,' Samantha's mother said quietly. 'And you know how it feels to come last, Maria. But it's up to you girls.'

Much later, Maria and Samantha sat on a front fence in the fading light. The street was almost empty now, just a few parents calling their children and some others collecting rubbish and pulling down the banner.

'Are you going to visit Rod?' Maria asked.

'Don't know.' Samantha stood up and yawned.

'Maybe we could visit him after the newspaper comes out … just in case he's missed our picture.'

'Good idea,' Maria said grinning. 'Oh, and I think I might train with you for next year's race. We'll start soon. Okay?'

Samantha nodded and, arms entwined, they walked off together.

'My legs might be even longer next year,' Maria commented, nudging Samantha with her hip. 'So watch out!'

Activities and Discussion

Win/Win

Ask the students to choose a situation from the story *Streaky Road Dash*.

Ask them to think about how the situation would produce a win/lose scenario and a win/win scenario for one of the characters in the story.

Ask the students to complete the activity sheet Decisions.

Personal Expectations

Ask the students to write a summary of their own level of determination to achieve their goals in the following areas:

▸ school and learning

▸ sport

▸ home

▸ friends

▸ family.

Rank the level of determination in the scale provided on the activity sheet Goals.

Determination

Introduce the topic by explaining that your values will help you decide how to act, how to live, how to treat other people and how to treat yourself. Your values influence the decisions you make.

Ask the students to complete the activity sheet Personal Values.

Is Winning Everything?

Ask the students to write or draw about a time when they were faced with a tough decision, as Samatha was in the race, for example, to help someone else and maybe forego your own reward. They can use the activity sheet Is Winning Everything?

Ask the students to explain the scenario in terms of: Win/Win and Win/Lose.

Decisions

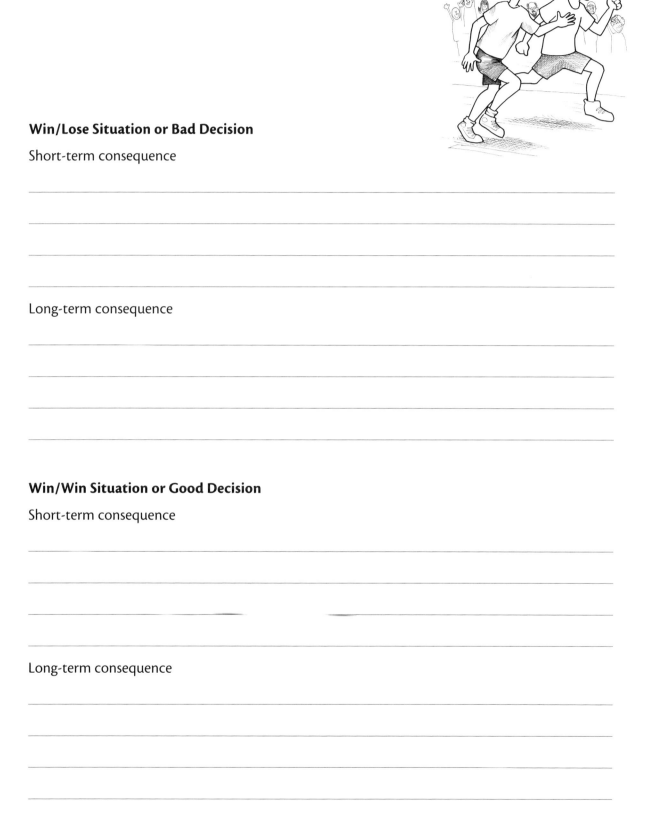

Win/Lose Situation or Bad Decision

Short-term consequence

_____

_____

_____

Long-term consequence

_____

_____

_____

_____

Win/Win Situation or Good Decision

Short-term consequence

_____

_____

_____

Long-term consequence

_____

_____

_____

Goals

Identify your goals in each of the following areas, and how determined you are to meet them on a scale of 1-10.

1 = not very determined and 10 = very determined

Area	Goal	Rating
School and Learning		
Sport		
Home		
Friends		
Family		

Do you believe that your expectations of yourself are responsible and realistic? Explain.

_____

_____

Personal Values

List your six most important personal values.

1. _____

2. _____

3. _____

4 _____

5. _____

6. _____

Describe a personal achievement whereby your success was influenced by one or more of your values and your level of determination.

_____

_____

_____

_____

_____

_____

_____

_____

_____

_____

Is Winning Everything?

Explain the scenario in terms of Win/Win and Win/Lose.

Win   **Win**

VS.

Win   **Lose**

How important is your attitude to a situation and your level of determination in achieving a positive win/win outcome?

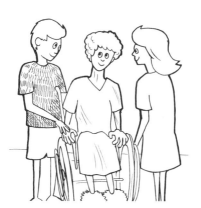

Objectives

▸ To help students become aware of the many people who require care in our communities.

▸ To identify the many forms Caring may take.

▸ To help students examine the importance of caring.

Factors Enhancing Resilience

▸ Promoting a sense of belonging and fitting in

▸ Recognition of a special talent or gift

▸ Enhancing a positive social orientation.

Introduction to the Focus Value

Brainstorm with the students and create a class definition of the focus value, 'caring'. The students may like to use a dictionary or thesaurus to assist in defining the meaning.

With the whole class, or in small groups, discuss how caring could be positively demonstrated in the classroom and the playground, and how they would know if it was not.

The Story: Nan's Place

The story may be read to the class by the teacher, or in small groups if multiple copies have been made.

Follow the story with a class discussion. Some suggested questions are:

▸ Where does the story take place?

▸ Why is Mrs Secree in a nursing home?

▸ What could be some of the reasons why people need to live in a nursing home?

▸ How did the twins, Hannah and Steve, react to having to visit their great grandmother?

▸ What was happening in the story that demonstrated Mrs Secree's need for care?

▸ Do you think that the twins and their mother were showing caring behaviour by visiting Mrs Secree each month? Explain.

▸ How do you demonstrate care for members of your family?

▸ Why do you think it is important for people to feel cared about?

Materials

▸ Families and Caring activity sheet.

▸ A Caring School activity sheet.

▸ My One Minute Talk activity sheet.

▸ Coloured pens.

▸ Hearts activity sheet.

nan's Place

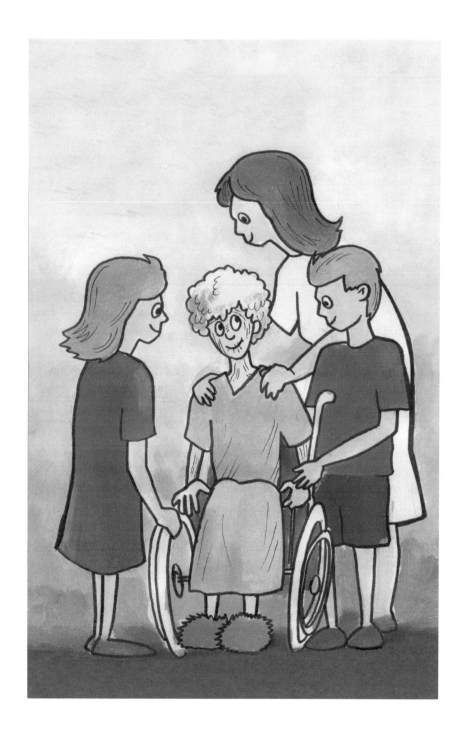

Written by Helen Silvester
Illustrated by Ian Moule

Chapter 1

'Now, Hannah and Steve, I don't want you to be rude to my nan.' The twins' mother stood facing them in the car park of the nursing home. 'I know her mind can wander a bit at times, but she's 99 years old and she is my nan. The least you can do is not look so bored.'

Hannah and Steve rolled their eyes at each other and nodded. They hated their monthly visit to see their mother's nan.

As soon as they walked in the door, the twins felt the overpowering urge to whisper. It was always so quiet, and the smell of disinfectant was everywhere.

'Sorry' the person on the reception desk apologised. Her usually quiet voice seemed louder than normal as she shuffled the paper lists in front of her.

'We're in a bit of a mess at the moment. They're starting the new conservatory today and we're all trying to get things done before they lay the foundations. Let me see. Your nan is Mrs Secree. I think she's in her room.' The receptionist frowned. 'She was a little restless this morning. The nurse was going to take her to the verandah to watch the workmen soon. Perhaps you could do that for her?'

When they got to her room, Nan was sitting at a small table piled high with old scrapbooks and photograph albums. She didn't hear them enter the room.

Chapter 2

'No, no, no,' she muttered as she turned the pages of the scrapbook in front of her. Every page was filled with old yellowed newspaper clippings.

'Nan?' said the twins' mother cautiously. 'Nan?' she repeated a bit louder.

Nan looked up. 'I can't find it. I just can't find it!'

'What can't you find, Nan?'

'The thing. You know, the thing. I just can't find it!'

Hannah and Steve felt embarrassed as they watched their mother try to comfort her tearful nan.

'Can we go, Mum?' Hannah looked pleadingly at her mother. 'We'll wait outside while you...' Hannah stopped as Mum frowned warningly in their direction, before turning back to her nan.

'It's all right, Nan. We'll help you look for it,' she said, putting an arm around her nan's fragile, stooped back.

Nan pulled away and frowned at them. 'Who are you? I don't know you. Nurse. Nurse!'

A casually dressed nurse came quickly into the room at Nan's call. Hannah recognised her by the layers of beads and necklaces she wore. The nurse nodded a greeting to Hannah, Steve and their mother.

'Now, Mrs Secree, you mustn't get yourself excited like that. It's just your granddaughter and her children come to visit you. How about we take them to the verandah so that you can all enjoy the fresh air.

Chapter 3

Nan calmed at the sight and sound of her favourite nurse. She allowed herself to be led to the verandah, with the twins hanging well back. It was all going well until Nan saw the workmen digging the hole for the foundations of the new conservatory.

'Mine!' Nan shouted suddenly. She grabbed at the nurse, getting handfuls of the beaded necklaces.

'Mine!' she yelled. The beads broke and rolled over the floor. 'Mine!'

The children's mother tried to untangle Nan's hands from the nurse's beads as Nan became increasingly upset.

As the twins watched, Nan tried to push her way along the verandah towards the workmen. Her fragile body seemed to grow stronger.

'Lets get out of here,' urged Hannah. She had had enough of being embarrassed by Nan's behaviour. Nan didn't even know who they were, so she would never miss them.

'Great idea,' Steve replied. 'Let's go in here until they take Nan back to her room.'

Steve opened some nearby doors and checked inside. The room was stacked with piles of clean linen. The nurse's green eyes stared accusingly at Steve and Hannah as the children shut the door to escape the fuss.

All at once, Steve and Hannah felt dizzy. The room seemed to toss and buck under their feet, as if it were spinning out of control. Their stomachs rebelled against the motion. Afraid they might throw up, they quickly reopened the door.

Chapter 4

Outside, everything had changed. People were screaming and jumping off the verandah, running towards a large hole in the middle of the lawn. The twins looked for their mother, but she was not on the verandah or in the crowd. Neither was the nurse.

'Look at their clothes,' said Hannah. The people, now crowded around the hole, were wearing old-fashioned clothing. The ladies had ankle length dresses, and the men wore either suits or pants with braces. In fact, everything around them looked like the seventy-year-old photos near reception. Thoroughly confused, Hannah and Steve stared at the crowd. Suddenly, a woman wailed in the centre of the crowd.

'My baby! My baby's fallen down a mine shaft.'

As everyone started shouting, a tall slim nurse, wearing a long white uniform, strode over the lawn towards the crowd.

'That's enough,' she said in a strong voice. 'Who's fallen where?'

At the sound of the nurse's voice, the crowd became silent and parted to allow her through.

'My baby, Nurse Elsie! The ground fell away beneath her! My baby's dead!' The mother began to wail again.

'Nonsense,' said the nurse. 'Jonathan, go and get your new car at once. Does anyone have some rope?'

Two men ran off, driving back a few minutes later in a shiny new car. But the car was as old-fashioned as the clothes they wore.

'Now, back it up near the hole and tie a rope around the bumper bar,' commanded Nurse Elsie, as she took off her hat and rolled up her sleeves.

The twins watched as she grabbed the rope and lowered herself into the hole.

Everyone held their breath. Suddenly, a weak cry came from the mine. Moments later, Nurse Elsie appeared with the child in her arms.

'Elsie Secree! How dare you risk yourself like that,' a severe matron yelled from the veranda.

Startled, the twins stepped back into the linen room to avoid being noticed by the matron.

Once more the room spun around them. Then they heard voices from outside.

'Elsie Secree! Please, sit down.' This time it was a quieter voice, of the nurse.

It was followed by their mother's voice begging, 'Nan, please sit down.'

When they opened the door and looked outside, the twins saw that the mine hole was gone. In its place were the workmen, digging with shovels and picks.

'Mine!' Again Nan's voice rang out over the veranda.

All of a sudden, everything fell into place for Steve and Hannah. Nan wasn't after the nurse's beads; she was trying to warn the workmen about the mine! The twins didn't question how they had seen what they had seen. All they knew was that their nan, Elsie Secree, was the nurse who had rescued the baby all those years ago, and now she was trying to stop another accident. She was just trying to warn the workmen about the mine!

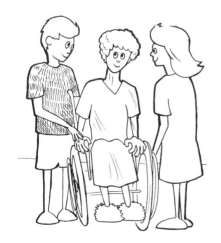

Hannah and Steve ran to their mother and explained about the mine. While Mum hurried to stop the workmen, Steve patted Nan's hand.

'It's all right, Nan. They know about the mine now.'

Nan smiled.

Families and Caring

Explain that families show caring in many different ways.

Ask the students to identify in words and pictures how their family shows caring towards them, on the activity sheet Families and Caring.

Caring For Each Other

Using the activity sheet A Caring School, ask the students to create a 'Caring For Each Other At School' brochure, that demonstrates what 'caring' looks like at their school.

Ask the students to think about the following questions when they are designing the brochure:

▶ Why is it important to care for each other at school?

▶ Why is it important to care for the school grounds as well?

Talking Care

Ask the students to create a one-minute talk about something they really care about. For example, it may be the environment family, sport or a hobby. Ask the students to each present their talk to the class explaining why caring is so important to them and how they demonstrate it.

Feeling Cared About

Explain to the students that all of us like to know we are cared about in some way. Using the Hearts activity sheet, ask the students to write about a time that someone showed they cared for them. Ask them to explain what happened.

Families and Caring

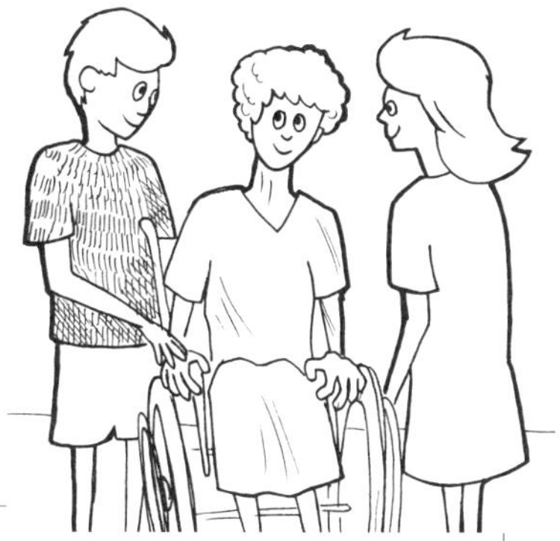

Using words and pictures identify how your family shows caring towards you, and how you show caring towards them.

My family cares for me by:

I care for my family by:

On the back of the sheet, write a 'How To Care For Me' set of instructions for your family to follow. List ten suggestions for them to follow that would demonstrate caring to you.

A Caring School

Design a brochure that demonstrates what 'caring' may look like at your school.

Caring at our school looks like..

My One-minute Talk

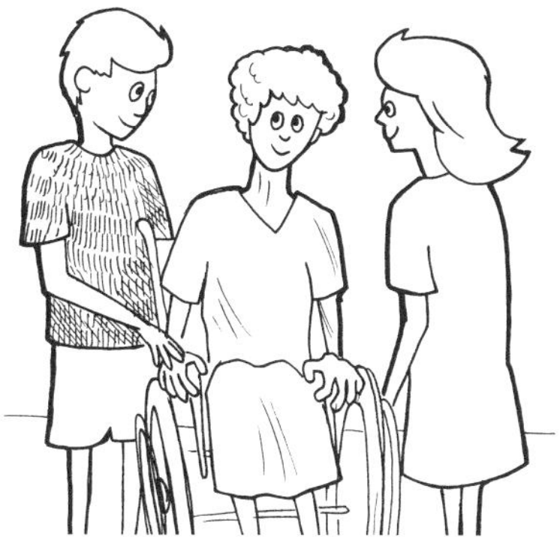

Make notes, and before your class talk you could practise with a partner – they could time you.

_____

_____

_____

_____

_____

_____

_____

_____

Design a front cover for a book about your 'caring' topic. Be sure to give it a title and suitable supporting illustrations.

Hearts

In the heart shape write or draw about a time when someone showed they cared for you.

Cut out the heart shape and place it onto a class display about caring.

Focus Value – Assertiveness

Objectives

▶ To help students identify the various forms that bullying can take.

▶ To help students identify behaviours and values that promote a sense of belonging.

▶ To help students examine the importance of assertiveness.

Factors Enhancing Resilience

▶ Promoting a sense of fitting in or belonging.

▶ Recognition of a special talent or gift.

▶ Promoting proactive problem-solving.

▶ Encouraging an optimistic sense of future.

▶ Enhancing a positive social orientation.

Introduction to the Focus Value

Brainstorm with the students and create a class definition of the focus value, 'assertiveness'. The students may like to use a dictionary or thesaurus to assist in defining the meaning.

With the whole class, or in small groups, discuss how assertiveness could be positively demonstrated in the classroom and the playground, and how they would know if it was not.

The Story: Slugger

The story may be read by the class teacher, or in small groups if multiple copies have been made.

Follow the story with a class discussion. Some suggested questions are:

▶ What does assertive behaviour look like at school?

▶ How was Priscilla assertive in the story?

▶ How would you react if Slugger was in your class?

▶ How is assertive behaviour different from aggressive and passive behaviour? Give examples.

▶ Why do people bully others? Explain.

▶ Priscilla used a number of assertive strategies with Slugger. What were they?

▶ Explain the saying: 'A wise person knows when to walk away from trouble.'

Materials

Assertiveness Strategies activity sheet.

Assertive Cube activity sheet.

Assertiveness Game activity sheet.

My Top Ten Assertive Actions activity sheet.

Slugger

Written by Jennifer Cooke
Illustrated by Katie Jardine

Focus Value – Assertiveness

Slugger

Written by Jennifer Cooke
Illustrated by Katie Jardine

I used to be a bully. There, I said it. I'm not proud of it, but when you've bullied as many kids as I have there isn't much use denying it.

As far as bullies go, I was pretty good at it. I'd tease kids for being too fat, too skinny, too smart, too good at sport, or too bad at sport. Any excuse would do: maybe their hair was too curly, their ears were too big, or their legs looked like they belonged on a chicken.

Maybe they talked strangely or talked too much, or didn't even talk at all. I'd tease them if they had a runny nose or if their shoes weren't as 'cool' as mine.

It didn't really matter what I chose, just as long as the person felt as if they were different from everyone else. Sometimes, I even made them cry. That meant I could call them a big baby, which was even better.

Lots of kids were scared of me, which is what I wanted, I suppose. It was great for my reputation as the biggest and baddest kid at my school.

What it wasn't any good for, was helping me to make real friends. You know, friends who like to hang out with me because I'm lots of fun. Not kids who hang out with me because they are frightened that I will beat them up if they don't play with me.

But it took me a while to figure that out. The funniest thing is that the kid who helped me understand this was the one I used to pick on most of all. Not that she ever seemed to notice, which made me madder than ever.

Her name was Priscilla, and she looked like she had walked out of a time machine. I mean, the girl wore blue cardigans knitted by her great-grandmother and long grey socks that pulled up to her knees.

Our school uniform hung off her like a big sack, and because her old granny had made it for her, it was way too long and sort of flared out at the bottom. She looked like she was wearing a big triangle.

OLD FASHIONED METAL MOUTH BRACES

CARDIGAN KNITTED BY A GREAT GRANDMOTHER

ALWAYS READING SOME HUGE BOOK

UNIFORM IS LIKE A BIG OLD SACK

BIG CLUMPY BLACK SHOES

LONG GREY SOCKS

Priscilla never wore sports shoes, just big clumpy black school shoes, because her feet were flat. And she had braces on her teeth. Not the new fancy type, which are clear, but the old-fashioned, metal mouth kind.

All in all, this girl just didn't fit in. She didn't look like anyone else and she didn't act like anyone else. She was perfect to pick on... or so I thought.

I tried everything to stir that Priscilla-gorilla princess up. I called her a teacher's pet in class and a clumsy cow in sport. I imitated her voice using the highest whingy whine that I could manage. I even pulled her hair once, when she was on the way to the library, and another time I accidentally-on-purpose threw a spitball at her.

But nothing would rattle this girl. She would just look through me as if I wasn't even there, and get on with whatever she was doing. Usually, that was reading some huge book or scribbling on a notepad. She was going to be a writer, or so she said. But when the teacher told her to stand up in class and read out her latest masterpiece, I sat up the back and made farting noises.

'Percy Underfield! If that is the most mature comment you have to offer on this subject, then you can stay back after school and consider your behaviour,' the teacher told me.

Then the kids laughed behind their hands at me, even Jack, Oliver and Max, and they were supposed to be my friends.

I hated it when people laughed at me, but with a name like Percy I had grown to expect it. That's why I had to be so tough all the time. If you have to go through life with a name as silly as I thought Percival was, then you'd better make sure you are as tough as nails.

Because I hated it when anyone said my real name, I made all the kids call me Slugger because that sounded like the name of someone you wouldn't want to mess with.

Only parents and teachers called me Percy. No one else dared to, except Priscilla. So I did what I always did when someone dared to annoy me. I waited after school behind the shelter shed to get back at her.

The only trouble was, Priscilla wasn't much of a challenge, being so skinny and small, and a girl and all.

I was telling this to my mates, Jack, Oliver and Max, when all of a sudden I was knocked flying by what looked like a giant ball of blue wool.

I couldn't believe it. Here I was, sprawled in the dirt spitting clumps of grass out of my mouth. Worst of all, I could hear people laughing.

'Oh Percy! I'm so sorry. Here, let me help you up,' I heard a panting voice say.

I was too stunned to say anything.

Before I knew it, Nancy-pants Priscilla-gorilla princess had her

paws all over me. And once again I could hear my so-called mates laughing at me.

So she had decided to get the jump on me, had she? Thought she'd strike the first blow? Well, I would show her.

'Get off me, you cow! I'm going to get you!' I roared.

Suddenly no one was laughing. Instead, Max and Jack were helping me up and Oliver was trying to tell me something. 'Slugger, she didn't mean it, honest. She just came racing around the corner and ran into you. Come on mate, she's just a silly girl,' Olly explained, trying to calm me down.

'I most certainly am not a silly girl, Oliver, and I am almost as certain that Percival doesn't really want to kill me, nor does he think I am a creature with four stomachs and a huge udder.'

Crikey, Priscilla could gab! She might not have meant to knock the wind out of me, but now she was having a really good go at talking me to death.

'Stop calling me that!' I was so angry that I could feel my face going all purple and splotchy, and I was even beginning to see stars.

'Oliver, Max, Jack, get lost. Priscilla-gorilla, you're coming with me.'

'What are you going to do, Slugger?' Max asked.

'Get her good, Slug. We'll wait for you,' Jack advised.

'Mate, she's not worth it. Leave it alone, will ya?' Oliver said.

'Go away!' I shouted. To be honest, I don't know why I told them to get lost. I usually liked my mates to see what happened to people who got under my skin, but this girl was something else. For a start, she kept using big words and talking like she was born a hundred

years ago. I was never sure if she was making fun of me or not. So I put on my biggest, toughest face, got up really close to her and said, very slowly and loudly so that there could be no misunderstanding, 'Don't call me Percy! The name is Slugger.' Well, she didn't even blink, although she did wipe her face where I had spat on her a bit.

Then she said in a quiet voice, 'You have no idea, do you? I mean you really don't know.'

'What are you talking about? Of course I know,' not knowing what on earth she was on about but not wanting to let on.

'Then why are you so upset that I called you Percival? It is such a great name that I thought you'd be proud to have it said out loud. I 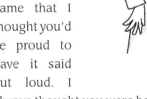 always thought you were being considerate of the other kids who had such plain names. I mean, some names really do show a lack of imagination.'

'Are you mad? The name Percy sucks! It's the closest you can get to a girl's name without actually being called a girl. It was my great, great uncle's name and it is some old family tradition, and I hate it. I hate it so much I could puke.'

'On the contrary, Percival is a name of great power. But clearly you don't know that, so I will tell you. Hundreds and hundreds of years ago there was a great king of Britain, called Arthur. He had a magician called Merlin and a whole lot of

great mates he called the Knights of the Round Table, because they used to sit at a big, round table,' Priscilla began.

'Fascinating,' I muttered.

'I'm glad you think so. Now, these knights used to travel around doing good deeds, slaying dragons, rescuing maidens and other stuff. But none was as brave or as loyal as King Arthur's knight, Sir Percival.'

'So what? That Percival sounds like a big girl if you ask me,' I said, but to tell you the truth she had me interested.

'Percival, I wish you'd stop saying 'girl' as if it's a bad thing. Never mind. No, Percival was most certainly not a girl, although that is a fine thing to be. Indeed, he was so brave and true that King Arthur gave him the most important job in the world to do: to find the Holy Grail.'

'The what?'

'The Holy Grail. It was a special cup that some people believe a holy man drank out of before he died. People have searched for it for years and years and years.'

'So Percy found it?'

'No, he didn't. For all we know, he is out there somewhere still looking for it. But that is the point, don't you see?'

'What? That he not only has a silly name, but he can't find a stupid old cup?'

'No, he never gave up his noble quest because he had made a promise to his king, and he was not going to let him down. Don't you see? He was not only brave and loyal, but he had a good heart. He was the most noble of men, and you, Slugger, share his name. I can't help but think that if you share his name, then you must share his power.'

Power? Me? Yeah right. I could feel my face going all hot like I was blushing, so I just turned around and ran off, leaving Priscilla standing there.

I ran all the way home, past Max, Oliver and Jack who were yelling out for me, past the shops where I liked to hang out after school, all the way to my street, and my house, and my room and my bed. Then I just lay there for a long time, thinking.

Now, I'm not saying that I suddenly thought I was this Sir Percy guy, but I had to admit, I had spent so long hating my name that it was a really big shock to find out that there was some good stuff about it. A lot of good stuff. Being a knight was cool. Those guys were tough, and yet, they helped people. That was a new idea to me.

The next day at school, I felt different: a bit taller. And I even grabbed a little kid's hand when he went to dart across the road before the school crossing lights had changed. He looked terrified, but I just told him to be careful and smiled at him.

The crossing lady said, 'Thanks Percy,' and I didn't even scowl at her. When I saw Max, Oliver and Jack waiting for me, I just walked up to them, all quiet.

'What did you do to Priscilla, Slugger?' Jack asked.

'Did you get her good, Slugger?' asked Max.

'That's between me and Priscilla, guys. I'm not going to talk about it. Not now, not ever.' They looked at me with their mouths wide open. Usually, I loved to talk about my fights, but not this time.

I looked past them and saw Priscilla standing a little way behind, off to the side, book open as always. But she was looking over at me. I didn't let her know I saw her.

Instead, I looked my mates straight in the eyes. 'And by the way, the name is Percival, or Percy. Never call me Slugger again.'

Then I walked off smiling, feeling tall and very proud of myself.

Activities and Discussion

Assertive Strategies

Discuss the differences between being assertive, passive and aggressive. Ask the students, in pairs, to complete the activity sheet Assertiveness Strategies.

Role-play

Ask the students, in pairs, to create a scenario about a bullying incident where they or their partner demonstrate the use of an assertive strategy to defuse a situation.

Ask the students to perform their role-play to the class if time allows.

Assertive Cube

Ask the students to make an 'assertive cube', using the Assertiveness Cube activity sheet. Ask them to write some possible assertive responses to a bullying situation on the cube.

Ask the students to throw the cube to practise some different ways to respond.

Use the scenarios below to help students use the cube and develop a variety of responses:

▸ A student wants you to bring money to school for them.
▸ A student keeps teasing you about your inability to catch a ball.
▸ A student calls you names.
▸ A student keeps pushing you when they see you.
▸ A student teases you because of the clothing you are wearing.

Being Assertive

Explain to the students that there are three basic ways to respond to a situation in which you are being bullied.

Type of Response	What it Looks Like
An aggressive response	Hitting, yelling, shouting, swearing.
A passive response	Give into others and let them continue to do bad things to you. – Crying – Mumbling.
An assertive response	Speak firmly, stand tall, stay in control of yourself.

Give some scenarios and ask the students to demonstrate a passive, aggressive and assertive response to each on. For example:

▸ Someone is threatening to take your lunch.
▸ A group of students are calling you names.
▸ A group of students are calling your friend names.

My Top Ten Assertive Actions

Discuss with the class, some actions that would support an assertive response to a bullying situation.

Ask them to create a list of suggested assertive actions that a younger student could take if they felt they were being bullied at school.

Distribute the activity sheet My Top Ten Assertiveness Actions. Working individually the students can rank the ideas into order of the most effective. Discuss the differences of ranking as a class.

Assertive Strategies

How did Priscilla demonstrate assertiveness in the story *Slugger*?

1. _____

_____

2. _____

_____

3. _____

Make a list of some assertive strategies you could use if you were being bullied by someone.

1. _____

_____

_____

2. _____

_____

3. _____

_____

4. _____

_____

5. _____

_____

Assertive Cube

Some ideas for the writing on the assertive cube are: walk away, tell someone, make a joke, stand tall, laugh it off or ignore them.

Assertiveness Game

Design a simple board game that promotes the use of assertive behaviours when being provoked. Include chance cards in your game. For example:

Assertive Chance Card

You stand tall and say 'No' firmly.

Advance 10 spaces.

Aggressive Chance Card

You are so angry you hit the other person.

Go back 8 spaces.

Passive Chance Card

You give in to the other person and let them continue to hurt you.

Go back 7 spaces.

Our ideas

_____

_____

_____

_____

_____

_____

_____

_____

_____

_____

If time allows turn your design into a real game.

My Top Ten Assertive Actions

Rank your ideas in order of the most effective.

1. _____

2. _____

3. _____

4. _____

5. _____

6. _____

7. _____

8. _____

9. _____

10. _____

▸ Rewrite a fairytale to show the value at work. You may like to give the fairytale a new twist!

▸ Create an acrostic poem about the value.

▸ Design a commercial for television promoting the benefits of practising the value at school or at home. (This could be done in small groups.)

▸ Design a word search of words relevant to, or associated with, the value.

▸ Make a show bag of items and gimmicks that could promote the value.

▸ Design a picture storybook for a younger audience to read that promotes the value.

▸ Design a comic strip that depicts the importance of practising the value. (Use your favourite comic character or invent you own character.)

▸ Create a list of ten hot tips for success using the value as a focus.

▸ Create a 'recipe' for the value. Remember to include the ingredients and the method in your directions.

▸ Design and make a CD cover listing 10 top song titles about the value, or change parts of the titles to promote the value.

▸ Design a personal shield or symbol that represents the value to you.

▸ Design a certificate to be used as an award for someone at your school who exhibits this value.

▸ Create a questionnaire to survey other students about the impact that practising of the value could have on the school. Graph your findings.

▸ Create a cartoon character and a slogan to promote the specific value.

▸ Interview students for an article about the value. Write the information as a newspaper item and present it to the grade as a news scoop!

▸ Interview teachers and record relevant stories that could be used as part of a classroom book.

▸ Invite a guest speaker to the school or grade, who has used the value to make a difference in the local community or someone's life.

▸ Interview parents about the importance of the value, or ask them to explain how the value has helped in their lives.

▸ Design a T-shirt that promotes the value.

▸ Find stories in the school library that focus on the value.

▸ Search newspapers and magazines for stories that illustrate the value. Design a class notice-board for their display.

▸ Conduct a unit of history research on a famous person who demonstrated the value. Report your findings to the class.

▸ Write to the local paper listing ideas that your local community could implement to help your area.

▸ Conduct a games session that promotes the value.

Bibliography

Benard, B. (1995) *Fostering Resiliency in Kids: Protective Factors in the Family, School and Community,* Western Centre for Drug Free Schools and Communities, Portland, Oregon.

Cahill, H. (1999) Why a Whole School Approach to Enhancing Resilience?, *Mindmatters Newsletter,* March, p 2.

Canfield, J. and Siccone, F. (1995) *101 Ways to Develop Student Self Esteem and Responsibility,* Massachussetts: Allyn and Bacon.

Cantor, R., Kivel, P. and Creighton, A. (1997) Days of Respect: *Organising a School-wide Violence Prevention Programme,* Hunter House, California.

Catalano, R. and Hawkins, J.D. (Ed) 'The social development model: a theory of antisocial behaviour'. In Hawkins J.D. (Ed) *Delinquency and Crime: Current Theories,* New York: Cambridge Publications.

Centre for Adolescent Health, (1998) *The Gatehouse Project: Promoting Emotional Well-being: A Whole School Approach- Team Guidelines,* Centre for Adolescent Health, Melbourne.

Department of Education, Victoria, (1999) *Framework for Student Services in Victorian Schools: Teacher resource,* Department of Education, Victoria.

DfES (2003) *Developing children's social, emotional and behavioural skills: a whole curriculum approach.* Primary National Strategy.

Fuller, A. (2001). Background Paper on Resilience presented to the Northern Territory Principal's Association (Australia).

Fuller, A., McGraw, K., Goodyear, M. (1998) *The Mind of Youth.* Department of Education, Melbourne, Australia.

Fuller, A. (1998) *From Surviving to Thriving: Promoting Mental Health in Young People,* ACER Press, Melbourne.

Goleman, D. (1995) *Emotional Intelligence – Why it matters more than IQ.* London, Bloomsbury.

Hawkins, J. and Catalano, R. (1993) *Communities that Care: Risk and Protective Focused Prevention Using the Social Development Strategy,* Developmental Research and Programmes Incorporated, Seattle, USA.

Lickona, T. (1997) *'Educating for Character: a comprehensive approach'* in Molnar (ed.) The Construction of Children's Character, University of Chicago Press, Chicago.

Olweus, D. (1995) *Bullying or Peer Abuse at School – facts and interventions.* Current Directions in Psychological Science, 4,6, p 196-200.

Resnick, M.D., Harris, L.J., Blum, R.W. (1993) *The impact of caring and connectedness on adolescent health and wellbeing.* Journal of Paediatrics and Child Health, 29.

Rigby, K. (1996) *Bullying in schools and what we can do about it.* ACER Press, Melbourne, Australia.

Seligman, M. (1995) *The Optimistic Child.* NSW: Random House Australia.

Smith, C., McKee, S. (2005) *Becoming an Emotionally Healthy School.* A Lucky Duck Book, Paul Chapman. London.

Taylor, M. (2000) *'Values Education: Issues and challenges in policy and school practice'* in M. Leicester, C. Modgil and S. Modgil (ed.), Education, Culture and Values, Vol 2, Falmer Press London.